A DELICATE DANCE

◇ A DELICATE DANCE ◇

*Sexuality, Celibacy, and Relationships
Among Catholic Clergy
and Religious*

SHEILA MURPHY

CROSSROAD • NEW YORK

1992

The Crossroad Publishing Company
370 Lexington Avenue, New York, NY 10017

Copyright © 1992 by Sheila Murphy

Printed in the United States of America
Typesetting output: TEXSource, Houston

Library of Congress Cataloging-in-Publication Data

Murphy, Sheila M.
    A delicate dance : sexuality, celibacy, and relationships among
Catholic clergy and religious / Sheila Murphy.
      p. cm.
    Includes bibliographical references.
    ISBN 0-8245-1159-X
    1. Celibacy—Catholic Church. 2. Sex—Religious aspects—Catholic
Church. 3. Monastic and religious life. 4. Catholic Church—
Clergy. I. Title.
BV4390.M87 1992
253′.2—dc20   91-44754
                                          CIP

CONTENTS

INTRODUCTION

DONALD J. GOERGEN, OP

Religion, society, and personality are all complex and multi-faceted realities. Any discussion of Christian celibacy and human sexuality must take all of them into account. Yet one book cannot be expected to do justice to all facets of these complex areas of human life. We must accept a particular work for the insights and assistance it provides. Sheila Murphy's experience and research provide such assistance and insights.

Let us first identify some issues of human growth, such as personal identity, adult development, sexual behavior, relationships, and self-awareness. Each of these affects our experience of celibate life and each is inseparable from our understanding of sexuality.

Personal identity comprises cultural, ethnic, religious, economic, professional, and family issues as well as issues of sexual identity. Sexual identity alone involves questions of biological sex, gender, social roles, and orientation. Gender alone is becoming an increasingly vast field of research. Religious identity is an issue of spiritual growth, institutional identification, and public life. In the Catholic tradition it may involve professional religious life or ordained ministry or both. Religious life itself is a very diverse reality involving issues of socialization, identification, and formation.

For a committed or vowed Christian celibate, religious identity is an essential integrating factor. One's deepest identity is one's religious identity. Other facets of personal identity take shape within this self-understanding.

Given our sociocultural context in the Western or first world, issues of human sexuality have become paramount in personal

◊ 7 ◊

and social life. Issues of gender and orientation are given extensive attention and even become preoccupying. Yet even these issues for a celibate man or woman, whether gay, lesbian, or straight, are only part of a constellation of factors that come together and are rooted in one's religious self. The religious and spiritual self is the deepest integrating and organizational factor in personal identity for Christian celibate people. Celibacy here is not something other than being human but rather a particular way of being human. In religious life today the issues of religious identity, spirituality, gender, and orientation are major concerns of those who struggle with identity issues.

But in addition to identity issues there are issues of adult human development. It has not been easy for Catholic moral teaching to incorporate this awareness, nor for some theologies of celibacy to do so. There can be two unhealthy extremes: viewing celibate chastity as some distant, almost unattainable ideal toward which we strive but which we never reach, or viewing religious profession or ordination as signalling a finished product, developmentally speaking.

Celibate chastity is not only an ideal. It is a call to live concretely in a certain way. The challenge of celibate life requires that we take seriously both our humanness and a commitment to integrity. True integrity requires integration, and integration takes time. Yet the process of becoming celibate cannot take lightly the fact that we are called to live for the sake of the gospel, a gospel that asks of us a total commitment.

On the other hand, growth in chastity cannot ignore the reality of adult developmental tasks, stages, and crises. Human and personal development cannot be limited to a period of initial formation that produces a finished product. It cannot be programmed. Rather, how is my religious identity and spiritual life deepening and do I see an impact of such on my way of being sexual? Spiritual life and sexual life interact and mature together.

The concept of continuing formation is just beginning to address these issues. Continuing formation does not imply that there are no criteria for human, sexual, and spiritual growth that must be met by the professed religious or ordained minister at the time of profession or ordination. But neither can we suggest that the truly formative experiences in our lives all take place before religious profession or ordination. The life of a celibate person is continuously formative. We continue to be formed by the dialectic between expectations and experiences — continually becoming a new person as a result of them.

Where then does sexual behavior fit into the life of a celibate person? A celibate person matures sexually as a single man or woman who is religiously motivated. Sexual integration remains an essential adult developmental task. Sexual feelings as such are neither immoral nor inappropriate for a celibate person. Feelings are ordinarily neither moral nor immoral. They are indicators of emotional experience. Yet one must learn to distinguish between feelings and behavior. Feelings are meant to be felt (not repressed or suppressed). Behavior, however, is an aspect of life over which we exert control. How we act out our feelings behaviorly is a moral concern.

Sexual maturity requires affective growth, comfort with an affective life, and appropriate physical expression of affect. Genital behavior is not an appropriate physical expression of affect for a celibate person. How to express affection and yet contain the direction it takes is an adult task. Genital lovemaking is not the only channel that sexual affect takes, although our culture may be permissive or confusing in that regard. Christian wisdom sees genital love as an expression of affect within a committed intimate partnership. It is precisely such partnerships or marriages that celibate men or women choose not to make. This is not to say they choose to forego intimate relationships, but intimate love need not necessarily be genital.

Celibate sexuality is not something given or inherited or received by osmosis. It is something learned, but not something put off to be learned later. It is integral to a healthy and mature celibate life. It develops as we learn how to relate to others as adult celibate women and men and as we struggle with our own self-awareness and self-esteem.

One of the more central issues in human life is that of human relationships. This is true of celibate life as well. And human relationships all have their sexual dimension. Our sexuality comes with us into our relationships. Being sexual ultimately means being relational, namely, that we are structured for others. We cannot be or become who we are by ourselves alone.

Celibate friendships, intimate human relationships, are central to celibate life. Intimacy is another adult human task. Celibates cannot claim to love everyone in general without loving some concrete people in particular. Friendship, while being a gift, is also a part of discipleship. Love of friendship is one form that Christian love takes, a form of love to be as much exemplified in celibate life as in conjugal life.[1]

Relationships are of many kinds. There are family, community, friends, professional contacts, people to whom we minister and those who minister to us. There are friendships between men and women, women and women, men and men.

Our capacity to relate maturely to others involves a number of issues, pains, and joys: capacity for commitment, communication, self-assertion, vulnerability, self-knowledge, jealousy, manipulation. None of these are issues that are foreign to celibate life. We can fear intimacy, be driven compulsively toward it, addicted to it, feel cheated by it, overrate it, be preoccupied with it. We learn how to love, how to be a friend, how to be a brother or sister, how to minister. Relationships are at the heart of humanness.

Relationships stir up the issues of gender, orientation, culture, and race. Relationships do not come as finished products. They are not commodities in a consumer society. They can be exploitative, manipulative, and competitive, or integrating and nourishing.[2] They are not pain free, ready made, or subject to unilateral control. Yet they are the source of much meaning in life, a gospel value, and affect as much as anything our sense of self.

Self-awareness or healthy self-love is another crucial area in human growth central to celibate life and sexual maturity. Self-concept or self-image plays a major role in all our lives. How we see ourselves or accept ourselves affects our behavior and our relationships. Self-esteem is influenced by our sexuality and vice versa. Healthy celibate life is rooted in a healthy self-acceptance. I can accept and be who I am. There is a freedom to be me. I need not prove something, exploit someone, or exaggerate my self-importance.

A healthy self-love is not a false, ego-centered, narcissistic love of self. It sees the value of self-giving and self-sacrifice. It does not make me be the center of attention nor does it fear attention. It has come to grips with the disowned, less desired, or wounded aspects of one's self. It can be both vulnerable and strong.

Insight into one's self develops with age. A celibate person continues to mature throughout life. He or she becomes wise, becomes courageous, becomes whole. He or she develops a capacity to love more universally, to have boundaries stretched, to be open to the stranger, to be less restricted by limiting identities. We become compassionate, generous, faithful, and grateful people — because we are always allowing ourselves to be healed, re-created, deepened. Self-growth flows into spiritual life — the heart of celibacy.

These issues that confront us are not issues of human growth alone but also of spiritual growth. To be human means to be a spiritual person, and to be spiritual we must be human. The one develops in proportion to the other. Spiritual identity is at the deepest core of self-identity. It is ultimately who I truly am. Although my spirituality is always shaped by particular religious traditions, spirituality cannot be identified with religion alone.

One of the great challenges to spiritual development in the United States today is to be able to distinguish spiritual life from psychological life, *pneuma* from *psyche*.[3] While these two are clearly inseparable, they are distinguishable. Psychic, intrapsychic, interpersonal, emotional, and mental life are the stuff of which much human growth is made. But in addition to our human relationships with other human persons, there is also our human relationship to God, our human experience of God, questions of ultimate meaning and destiny, myth and symbol, faith and unbelief: humankind's specifically religious concerns.

Religious celibacy is ultimately only understood in the context of these religious questions, humanity's religious search, our spiritual quest, a spiritual self-understanding. One cannot make an authentic human choice for celibacy without addressing and facing the many psychological and social factors involved in human motivation. But at some point one needs to be able to pass through those issues to another level where the human person encounters God.

However our religious traditions shape our language about God, or allow us to articulate our experiences of God, God is at the heart of a celibate person's life and decision. Our experiences of God are commensurate with our human capacity for God and our human maturity. The Judeo-Christian traditions talk about a God who calls (Abraham and Sarah), a God who gets close (Moses), a God who sends us on mission (the prophets), a God who is with us (Jesus, Immanuel). A Christian celibate sees his or her life in the context of this interaction with his or her God. This struggle of self with Self, as a response to God, to grace, is one more story in the history of salvation, of God's presence to people.

Although many complex factors play a role in human life, these do not make the God factor insignificant. I am not defined by myself alone. I cannot be understood apart from God, who is part of my self-definition. Christian celibacy is a response to the gift of the Spirit. Christian celibacy places one's life in the history of that tradition of following after Jesus.[4] Christian celibacy is choosing to live "for the sake of the gospel." One cannot understand celibacy apart from this call of the gospel, apart from a soul thirsty for gospel, apart from this human yearning for self-transcendence.

The God of Jesus is a God of love and a God of power, a God whose power is the power of love, a God who is self-communicating and self-revealing, a compassionate, challenging, faithful, and generous God.[5] Who is the God to whom we have given over our lives? The celibate's ability to respond to God is not fundamentally different from or more profound than that of any other baptized Christian. Celibacy is simply the shape that his or her response to God takes.

Unable to explain his or her life in ordinary terms, the celibate is pushed or pulled beyond more common human categories in order to make sense of his or her life. The Christian celibate, like Paul, cannot not speak about the gospel.

All of this could go further. We must let go of it for now. A "spirituality" that is rooted in "gospel," a spirituality that is both human, humane, whole, holistic as well as "of God," is the natural habitat in which celibate people live their lives. Apart from the Spirit, the celibate person is like a fish out of water. Celibacy cannot be understood apart from the Spirit. It is not my task to develop further such a spirituality here but only to call attention to it.[6]

At this point something important must be said. Religious celibacy both flows from an internal freedom and contributes to it. Unfortunately many Roman Catholic priests find themselves in a position that is not freeing in this regard, given the obligatory character of clerical celibacy. And unfortunately, when many people think of celibacy they think of clerical celibacy, which may be a less effective witness to the meaning of true, freely chosen celibacy. This does not mean that there are not many diocesan priests who freely choose celibate life and effectively witness to its value. But there are also many for whom celibacy has not been freely chosen. This makes its meaning and value ambiguous.

Thus we have come to an important distinction between an obligatory celibacy and freely chosen, nonobligatory celibacy, between clerical celibacy and celibacy as understood within the context of religious life. They cannot be assumed to be the same. And the prime analogate or supreme exemplification for true celibacy is celibacy in the context of religious life. A freely chosen celibacy has spiritual power and apostolic value.

This true celibacy has traditionally been associated with mission, mysticism, and witness. One person's celibacy is not precisely the same as another's. Motivation is complex. There are many psychological, socioeconomic, and cultural factors. These cannot be denied. The celibacy of one particular religious family is not precisely the same as that of another. Monasticism differs from later apostolic traditions. The celibacy of a monk or nun serves a different purpose from that of a friar or a sister. Celibacy is intrinsic to the tradition of common life. But we need not pursue further this rich diversity in celibate life except to acknowledge it.

A great challenge facing celibate men and women in the Roman Catholic tradition today is the tension between an institutional role and a charismatic vocation as well as the tension between a public role and personal life, especially as that public role becomes more and more identified with the institution. These tensions contain many unarticulated issues.

Christian celibacy by nature is more of a call from God than it is a particular public office in the Church, a call better situated in the Church's charismatic traditions and tradition of religious life. Already in ancient Israel there were "charismatic" public religious roles and "institutionalized" public religious offices, although these ought not to be defined over against each other. Religion necessitates a variety of roles. Prophecy and wisdom, or the prophet and sage, were charismatic, religious institutions less capable of regulation due to their sense of more immediate accountability to God, human experience, and rationality. The priesthood and monarchy, or priest and king, were public religious institutions whose roles were more readily defined or prescribed. In each case one's loyalty and integrity would be understood differently — that led to conflict among them.

Celibacy strikes me as a charism that not only is less capable

of institutional definition but also as one that requires greater freedom or less regulation in order to be what it truly is at its best.
Priesthood on the other hand is clearly an office in the Church
that carries with it an accountability and loyalty to the Church
as an institution. Hence the tension that exists between celibacy,
priesthood, and religious life, or between a more freely chosen
celibacy and a more regulated clerical celibacy. Celibacy requires a
greater degree of freedom in order to be what it really is, which is
fundamentally a spiritual reality rooted in spiritual life. This does
not suggest by any means less responsibility, less of an ecclesial
sense, or less integrity, simply different calls, vocations — which
can overlap but do not necessarily do so. Religious life itself is already the institutionalization of a charismatic spiritual heritage of
which celibacy is a significant component. Religious life, in its renewal and in its obedience to the directives of the Second Vatican
Council, has questioned whether the renewal of celibacy does not
require its liberation from being obligatory for diocesan clergy.

Priests and religious today, women and men, feel this tension
in some form. How do I integrate public and personal life? Who
are the various publics to whom I am accountable? How do I see
my relationship to bishop or religious superior? What shape ought
leadership in our Church take today? How do I as a public person
in the Church understand and cope with the present leadership in
the Vatican? How do I minister in a divided Church? How are the
varied facets of Church held together? When does diversity become
divisive? What roles do compromise, confrontation, and reconcili-
ation play in Church life? How do I see my celibacy as constitutive
of my vocation and how do I see my vocation in relationship to
the Church as it is structured? Celibacy requires freedom. How do
I experience this freedom, and for what purpose? There are many
"celibates" who have not "chosen" celibacy. How do we evaluate
this fact?

These are not the only conflicts that are part of a celibate person's contemporary experience. There is the conflict between a
permissive society and a litigious society, between a liberal society
and a conservative Church, and between the Church's progres-
sive social teaching and conservative sexual ethics. Celibate men
and women come to adulthood and sexual maturity in an increasingly affluent and permissive Western society. One of the effects
of this affluence and permissiveness, however, has been a grow-

ing recourse to law and civil suits. Western society has become increasingly emphatic about democratic values, while at the same time the Roman Church has at least temporarily developed a policy of increased centralization. The same Church has become more inductive and pastoral in its response to social, political, economic, and ecological issues, while refusing to see the concerns of women and sexual minorities as also social issues. And there is the continuing debate between moral values and public policy in a secular and pluralistic context. These issues require of religious professionals tremendous maturity and balance. We are supposed to be human, but not too human. We are supposed to become human but not make mistakes. We are supposed to have personal integrity, social acceptability, and ecclesial loyalty. We are supposed to be socially conscious, professionally competent, and ecclesially committed. The expectations are not the same as fifty years ago, but they are high and they create stress.

Religious life and priesthood have been affected by the AIDS crisis. There has been a growing sensitivity in society to clerical misconduct. Ministering persons often find themselves in public roles with high expectations and minimal respect. Much of this also flows from the increasingly ideological polarization of Western society and Western religion. Ideological commitments more often than not co-opt the gospel. Yet the Christian celibate's ultimate commitment is to God and God's gospel. Celibacy is in the end a human response to spiritual values — fundamentally a spiritual reality that implies a commitment to profound spiritual growth. Celibacy cannot be understood or its meaning adequately articulated in any other context. But neither can celibacy deny the challenges of ordinary human growth. The celibate person is a spiritual person struggling to be human as much as a human person struggling to be holy. To understand its deeper meaning one must go in search of the gospel.

In this book Sheila Murphy sheds further light on this celibate journey toward the human, the holy, the sexual, and the celibate. She contributes to our courage and to our wisdom.

A DELICATE DANCE

Chapter 1

THE STORY

The only way to grow as a true human being is to take the risk of being a friend and giving time to establishing a friendship. Nothing is more important to the Church or to our world than friendship. Real growth can only occur in the human heart when there is a supportive relationship. (ORDER CLERGY, AGE 53)

My best friend (another brother in my community) and I are very close. It's amazing how much we mean to each other, how much we trust in and rely on each other. We work in different places, so we do our best to get time alone by registering for the same conferences and workshops and retreats. We're both gay, and have struggled with that. We're also both very committed to our congregation and our ministry. What we have in friendship is so good and so valuable that it couldn't possibly be wrong. Are we the only ones? Are there others like us? (BROTHER, AGE 36)

_____ and I have been best friends for over thirty years. We prioritize time together for movies, dinners, picnics, etc. He's as committed to his priesthood as I am to my religious life. Prayer is an important part of what we share. We are loving and affectionate, but have never had sex (not that there weren't tense times!). My only regret is that I don't feel free to talk about him with anyone because of the chances of misunderstanding and scandal. (SISTER, AGE 60)

When I vowed celibacy over twenty years ago, I never dreamed I'd be where I am now: in love, sexually active, ashamed, and elated. Am I the only one? What have others done who find themselves in this type of situation? (SISTER, AGE 42)

Four voices, four relationships, four struggling, questioning, celebrating, and searching vowed celibates who risk violating the ultimate taboo in traditional clerical and religious life circles — discussing their relationships, sexuality, and celibacy. Four women and men who admit they are still "in process" say, "These are our stories and experiences. Are we the only ones? Can we ever talk about this? Have others raised these questions? How have they worked through the dilemmas?"

Though often feeling alone and lonely in their struggle for authentic living of their religious lives, they are, in fact, not unique. Their company is legion: the sister who wonders if she should leave religious life because she does not know what to do about falling in love for the first time at age forty-six; the brother who has never had a "best friend" and questions his recently discovered attraction to a parishioner; the priest who has affairs and finds he can no longer tolerate the guilt; the sister who questions her sexual orientation and asks if there are support groups for "people like me"; the priests, sisters, and brothers who discover, as adults, that they are survivors of childhood sexual abuse and question the validity of their vows made at a time when they did not have "memories." Their company includes women and men who agonize over the role of intimacy in their lives — people who, as vowed celibates living during the second half of the twentieth century, discover that the pat answers and clear proscriptions of their early formation training simply do not work in post–Vatican II Church and society. Sharing the oppression of the "conspiracy of silence" when they want to talk about what they are going through, they bear the burden of isolation, believing they are the "only ones." Frustrated, they do not feel free to discuss what is most important to them.

This is a book about what some vowed celibates today are saying about their journeys in relationship, sexuality, and celibacy. It is a presentation of their experiences, questions, failures, and successes. As an initial attempt toward a type of "open forum" where questions are posed and discussion begins, it is an effort to reassure the thousands of vowed women and men — those struggling through adulthood with questions their parents and formation directors never prepared them for — that they are not alone, pathological, mixed up, or abnormal. It is *not* a book about morality, theology of the vows, or sexual ethics, nor is it a book with answers about how vowed celibates should be relational, sexual, or celibate. This text is germinal — the first planting inviting vowed celibates to talk with one another. How they tend the yet undefined seedling is up to them, but the hope is that initial discussion generates additional reflection and sharing.

Before outlining where the material for the text came from, I'd like to explain how I got involved as midwife to this conversation.

My Background

I am a single lay woman in the throes of midlife transition who grew up through the parochial school system of the 1950s and 1960s, so I experienced pre–Vatican II Church and society as backdrops to my youth. I met many priests and nuns through Church activities, CYO camps and athletics, and school, took my religion seriously, and eventually entered a religious congregation in the mid-1960s. I was not there long (I left during novitiate), but long enough to feel the first rumblings of change precipitated by Vatican II. After leaving the Dominicans, I continued in Catholic schools for my undergraduate (University of Dayton) and graduate (Boston College) degrees. The benefits were twofold: an excellent education and an appreciation for both pre– and post–Vatican II Church and society.

Never did I dream that I would spend the majority of my professional career working with vowed celibates and, even more, never did I dream that I would work with them in the areas of relationship, sexuality, and celibacy. I can only shrug my shoulders and say, "It just sorta happened!" Returning to the Midwest after graduate school, I was asked to conduct psychological testing for formation candidates in the Cleveland and Youngstown dioceses since I had some familiarity with religious life. From there, I was asked to provide counseling for formation candidates, then for professed religious, and before long I had a private practice consisting entirely of vowed celibates. Reflecting on what I was learning from these clients, I submitted articles to *Review for Religious*, *Sisters Today*, and *Human Development*, all of which stimulated invitations to speak to groups of religious and clergy in a variety of settings. I was definitely invested in ministers and their lives.

Concomitant with my private work was my employment as a professor at a small Midwestern Catholic college where I developed courses in human development, human sexuality, and gender studies. Several years ago, I combined the academic and the clinical in original research with women religious in midlife transition, a study precipitated by midlife sisters' questions in counseling: "Am I the only one going through this? Is this normal? How have others navigated these waters?" Exposure through *Midlife Wanderer* brought me into contact with an ever-widening circle of religious and clergy and their concerns.[1]

Over time, I noticed that women and men religious, as well as diocesan clergy, were asking more and harder questions about relationships, sexuality, and celibacy and fewer questions about stress and communication skills. I also noticed that their experiences were not always "typical" of those reported for men and women in general in the literature on adult development, sexuality, and gender studies.[2] In many respects, vowed celibates were enjoying much healthier and more intimate relationships than those reported for women and men in general; in other ways, they were less relationally mature. "What's going on here?" I asked, "And why?"

For example, numerous developmental psychologists have reported that men in our culture do not have best friends and, if they do, tend to name a woman (generally a spouse).[3] The brothers and priests I was seeing *did* report best friends who were fairly evenly divided between men and women. Unlike men in general who have "buddies" and "pals" with whom they discuss "things" and share "events," the vowed men revealed loving, meaningful relationships with friends with whom they shared prayer, values, theology, and philosophy of life.

Celibate women, on the other hand, were similar to women in general in that they claimed a best friend, generally another woman.[4] What was interesting was that so many of the women religious named other vowed celibates as their best friend. Another point: Vowed women and men claiming best friends grew up through novitiates and seminaries professing very clear proscriptions against that very phenomenon. How did they integrate, ignore, or transcend their early training? What about those who could not, such as the 46-year-old sister who offered this comment:

Relationships — at least long-term relationships — were not supported in the early 1960s when I entered. Our mobility and our "presumed ability" to be detached in relationships leave me with an insecurity about long-term relationships. That, coupled with cultural norms about "throwaway" *everything*, makes long-term commitment questionable.

Celibate women and men struggled to maintain their relationships over time, even after they moved from the house, ministry, or town where they initially met their friends. Regular contacts through visits, letters, and phone calls were frequently priorities when juggling budgets and vacations.

Quality time spent in quality conversation was another commonly articulated priority. Fun, certainly an important relational component, was secondary to meaningful sharing of ideas, beliefs, and values. In the same vein, "being together" superseded "doing together."

Vowed celibates appeared to share a broader definition of sexuality than do women and men in general. While most adults tend to equate sexuality with genital behaviors,[5] vowed celibates often endorsed more holistic approaches, claiming the full gamut of feelings, thoughts, and behaviors as potentially sexual.[6] As one 52-year-old sister said, "I've been very sexual with my best friend of the past twelve years in the intimacy of our sharing and the tenderness of our touch. We've shared many late nights with much holding and being for each other. Yes, I've been very sexual, but I've never had intercourse." This theme was repeated often by other vowed celibates, male and female. It seems they were willing to admit to a level of vulnerability and risk because they sensed relationship and sexuality were far more complex and rewarding than what they had learned about them in their high schools and novitiates and seminaries.

Needless to say, vowed celibates have no magic formula for successful relational growth that somehow removes them from the birth pangs of this unique developmental process. Their struggles to understand and to participate in meaningful intimacy consistent with their vowed status and community lifestyle are as numerous and varied as the individuals involved and frequently generate guilt, anxiety, and self-doubt. Some wonder if time devoted to a relationship is time taken from ministry or community interaction —

where, they learned during formation, their energies "should" be focused; some, embarrassed by never-before-experienced bouts of jealousy, assume they will never grow beyond adolescent-like crushes. And for most, questions surrounding the role of affectional and sexual expression within their primary relationships abound. It is no surprise, then, that "I must be wrong!" "This isn't worth it!" and "Does anyone else ever go through this?" are frequently heard laments from people in process.

This Book

What I was learning about relationships and sexuality through my academic preparations, combined with the stories and questions of vowed celibates with whom I interacted in counseling and workshops, coalesced into a logical realization: It was time to ask vowed people themselves about their own understandings of and struggles with the issues. Were my clients lone voices aberrantly crying in the wilderness or were they representative of other vowed celibates working toward authenticity in intimacy? Was it just my personal hunch or a verifiable fact that priests and religious were less bound by cultural stereotypes of how "real men" and "real women" experience relationships and sexuality? How do vowed women and men define celibacy today, and what does that mean in terms of their living out of their communal, ministerial, and relational lives? As I discovered during my study of midlife women religious, many professionals are willing to speculate and theorize about how diocesan priests and religious "should" live their lives, but too few have gone directly to the source to ask the obvious questions. Since I qualified for a sabbatical from my college, I decided I would use the time to fashion a forum in which vowed celibates could begin to talk with one another and with the professionals with whom they work about their lives as relational, sexual, celibate people in process.

I used two tools to establish a context for the discussion: a standardized psychological inventory, the *Bem Sex Role Inventory*, and an original eleven-page questionnaire in open-and closed-question format to solicit vowed celibates' attitudes and behaviors regarding relationship, sexuality, and celibacy. First, a few words about the *Bem*.[7]

Sandra Bem developed the paper-and-pencil self-report *Bem*

Sex Role Inventory to measure the extent to which individuals report themselves comfortable with culturally defined masculine and feminine responses. Respondents rate themselves on this adjectival checklist, and resulting scores are categorized into one of four groupings: psychologically masculine, psychologically feminine, neither, or both — androgynous.

Researchers working with the *Bem* have generated some provocative data.[8] For example, they have found that men and women who are successful in traditional masculine occupations such as management and accounting come out masculine on the *Bem*. Counselors and social service providers of both genders tend to come out feminine. Some of the most promising research, however, centers around persons who come out psychologically androgynous, as persons reporting themselves to be comfortable expressing the full gamut of human response, whether it is stereotypically "appropriate" to their gender or not.

Androgyny comes from the Greek roots *andros*, meaning male (as in "androgens") and *gyn*, meaning female (as in "gynecology"). Psychological androgyny results when people report themselves to be comfortable behaving in both stereotypic masculine and feminine ways, depending upon the demands of the situation. They can be direct when necessary, and can be empathic when needed as well. They can work well either alone or with others; they are less threatened than strong masculine or feminine types by people who do not exhibit behaviors of "real men" and "real women" in the cultural understandings of those words. Because of the flexibility of their response repertoire, psychologically androgynous people are considered mentally healthier than those locked into more rigid stereotypic behaviors.

As part of her doctoral dissertation, Jean Alvarez found her sample group of women religious to be more androgynous than women in general;[9] to date, I know of no comparable study conducted with either diocesan clergy or men religious. I used the *Bem* for two reasons: (1) to see if I could replicate Alvarez's study with a group of contemporary women religious and (2) to see how a sample group of diocesan clerics and men religious would come out on the inventory. If, in fact, androgynous persons transcend social stereotypes when situations demand it, would they also transcend culturally prescribed masculine and feminine conditioning for relationships? Might a relationship exist between psychological androgyny and freedom to be intimate in authentic development within celibate commitments?

The second tool, an eleven-page questionnaire, was an original document based upon research reporting men's and women's experiences of relationship, sex, and sexuality. I drew questions investigating attitudes toward celibacy from contemporary theologians, philosophers, and spiritual directors regarding various interpretations of celibacy throughout the ages.

The *Bem* is an accepted standardized instrument with an accompanying manual of research history and standardization procedures, but my questionnaire was original, so I needed to ascertain its acceptability, appropriateness, and completeness. I submitted it to psychologists active on ethics committees in professional mental health associations for their approval, which I received. I also asked a few men and women religious as well as some professors versed in relationship studies to check the questionnaire for thoroughness and clarity. The result represents their suggestions for modifications, but is solely my responsibility. Copies of the cover letter and the questionnaire, including results reported as percentages, are included at the conclusion of the text. I was pleased to receive the endorsement of Peggy Nichols, CSJ, of the Religious Formation Conference for the study.

The focus of the text is not the statistics generated by the two tools, but the trends, directions, stories, struggles, and questions they represent. Straightforward reporting of statistical data can be dull; creative exploring of what the numbers might mean is challenging and exciting and what this text is all about. Where appropriate, numbers and percentages will be woven into the material; otherwise, statistics will be relegated to end notes.[10]

Convincing vowed celibates to contribute their voices to this initial conversation was predictably difficult. Ideally, I should have contacted every diocesan cleric and man and woman religious in the country to participate. Limited resources precluded that option immediately. Given monetary and time constraints, I arbitrarily limited the respondent pool to vowed celibates between the ages of 35 and 65. My reasons for selecting this age range were twofold: (1) I needed to limit the respondent group somehow, and age was a convenient restriction; (2) I wanted to hear from women and men who had experienced pre–Vatican II Church and society, who had grown into early adulthood during post–Vatican II transitional

years, and who are maturing into middle adulthood and early preretirement while striving to integrate early training with changes
in the Church, living through the sexual revolution, experiencing
contemporary emphasis on relational similarities and differences
between women and men, and grappling with predictable adult
developmental transitions.

I decided, after considering time and finances, to aim for a respondent sample of 250 women and 250 diocesan clerics and men
religious, and distributed materials accordingly. The final tally of
returned materials came to 236 women and 97 men; of the men,
31 were diocesan priests and 66 were members of religious congregations — 26 brothers and 40 priests. The average age of the
women was 50 years and of the men, 47.[11]

Respondents were self-selected: they heard about the study and
agreed to participate. Without doubt, such a group is not necessarily representative of all vowed celibates, which raises several
important questions: Why would *these* people choose to participate? Why did some choose *not* to participate? Why did so many
men agree to respond then fail to return completed materials? Answers to these would generate interesting insights, but remain
unknown at this time.

Respondents were from twenty-seven states and two Canadian
provinces. I limited geographical area to the United States and
Canada because they are the two countries in which most relationship, sexuality, and celibacy research has been conducted. Ideally,
future investigators with more resources will pursue cross-cultural
investigations with truly random samples, which will certainly
enrich our understandings of human growth and development
among vowed celibates worldwide.

The voices speaking throughout the text are of ministers in a
variety of settings: inner-city projects, rural parishes, suburban
schools and churches, diocesan administrative offices, congregational administrations, retreat work, social service, and individual
study programs.

I invited comments on the questionnaire, and I quote respondents where I have their explicit permission to do so. Actual
scenarios presented in the text are disguised compilations of many
people and places for the purpose of confidentiality. The primary
content of the examples, however, is retained.

As ever, no work is a solo flight, and this is especially true in this relationally rich endeavor. Four special people from Canton, Ohio, deserve specific mention. Sandra Lopez-Baez, Ph.D., and Penny Bove, Ph.D., provided valuable input about and reactions to the questionnaire; they both brought enormous amounts of research in relationships to their critiques as well as personal and professional support. Ernest Paquet, FIC, kept me sane with his computer expertise, and John McKeon, Ph.D., provided rich statistical consultation and advice.

Many people gave generously of their time and energy in distributing packets of materials. They were Gary Adams, Ph.D.; Bernie Baltrinic, OP; Maria Beesing, OP; Thomas Bouterie; Bill Burkert, ST; Michael Crosby, OFM Cap; Jean Dezort, OP; Mary Ann Flannery, VSC; Tom Gedeon, SJ; Harold Grant, Ph.D.; Barbara Hammrel, OP; Jo Ann Haney, OSF; Mary Jakubiak, OP; Don Kimball; Bernie LoCoco, FCS; Bill McCool; Pat O'Leary, SJ; Kay O'Malley, SND; Christine Rody, VSC; Jan Schlichting, OP; and Loughlan Sofield, ST. I realize many others distributed packets to friends without my seeking the favor; while I do not know everyone involved, please accept my grateful thanks.

I extend a precious personal and professional appreciation to the four people I respect most for their contributions to the ongoing explorations of vowed celibates seeking meaningful intimacy, sexuality, and celibacy. They invested the time and energy to read and comment on an early draft of this material — Don Goergen, OP, Jeannine Gramick, SSND, Cornelius Hubbuch, CFX, and Sandra Schneiders, IHM. I hope I have incorporated their comments and suggestions well into this later rewrite.

A special thanks goes to all the women and men who gave of their time and selves to complete the *Bem* and the questionnaire. That many of you invested hours was evident from the lengthy comments you wrote. I thank you for all the women and men who will learn and benefit from your honesty and risk-taking. I also wish to thank the numerous unnamed clients who trusted me with their life stories while they searched for peace with themselves, others, and God. Know that I carry the lessons of your sacred journeys into this endeavor, and thank you for your contribution.

Finally, I want to thank three special Dominican women for their part in opening this dialogue. Donna is the unsuspecting Muse who unknowingly bumped me out of many episodes of ennui. Mary is my friend of more than fourteen years who patiently edited and corrected an earlier draft of the text; she taught me much about the hard coin of maturing, and it's reassuring to know that I finally carry a few pieces of that currency in my developmental pocket. Barbara is my friend with the fragile and ferocious heart who had the courage to say, "Murphy, get the hell out of the way and the book will write itself!"

Chapter 2

INTRIGUING INTIMACY

Real relationships require commitment, time, and effort and involve compromise and negotiation. This is difficult but rewarding. My relationships have had a humanizing effect on me, helping me to love, share life deeply, continue to grow, and find a deeper relationship with God. (ORDER PRIEST, AGE 58)

Friendships are the best thing in the world that have happened to us as religious! They [my relationships] have been very supportive. I have been able to survive long years in community/province administration only because of support of friends. Support has been mutual, also enjoyable! [They have] shown me how to relax and be my best and true self. It is important to know you are loved! (SISTER, AGE 64)

I am not sure why I am not filled with guilt over these relationships. Sometimes I feel that maybe I should be but I am not. I did go for counseling during the second relationship because it had gone on for a long time, I knew I had to get out of it, but I wasn't sure what I would be like without this person. . . . I have been four years without falling in love again. I don't feel I was less a religious when I was in these relationships. I felt my prayer life was good, my relationships with my sisters were good, and my work in my ministry was good. Things continue to go well for me. I sometimes miss the "high" of being in love. These people were very instrumental in helping my self-knowledge and building my self-esteem. I feel I grew because of our interactions. To have someone love you for yourself is one of the best presents God can give you. And I love my God even more because He has stayed with me through it all. I have no plans for falling in love again. But I had never planned on the other three. There was a magnetism there that I cannot explain and they just happened. They were not painless experiences but they were not unhappy experiences. I think I am the person I am today because of them. I have more growth to do as anyone has, but I am happy with where I am. (SISTER, AGE 48)

The men I have shared a rectory with and ministered with have not been "best" friends. I would like to have a "best" friend relationship with someone I share a home with. (DIOCESAN CLERIC, AGE 54)

Just what is it that makes the intimacy of a "best friend" so special, and how do contemporary vowed celibates fashion their lives to incorporate such intimacy into their community and ministerial commitments? Do men and women approach these differently? How do they define intimacy and live it out within the context of their relationships?

To answer these, we must first face some cultural and personal ambiguities surrounding the definition of intimacy. Just what is it? Straightforward dictionary definitions offer some clues: inmost, inner, essential — something deeply personal and private not readily accessible to others on superficial observation. To describe a relationship as intimate, then, is to suggest that something unique and personal undergirds what two people share. *What* is being shared and called intimate, however, is not always clear.

A commonly accepted understanding of intimacy in contemporary culture is that intimacy equals sex, so when someone says, "I got intimate with so-and-so last night," we are quite clear about what she or he is telling us. Another variation on the same theme is reflected in the warning so many vowed celibates heard during their formation, "It's okay to be friendly with another, just don't get intimate." References to the "intimate bond" or the "intimacy of marriage" clearly underscore the "intimacy equals sex" equation. Social scientists such as Michael McGill and Lillian Rubin have determined that men, much more than women, endorse this understanding.[1] Such interpretation renders intimacy identifiable and quantifiable, but fails to convey the totality of many people's, both men's and women's, experiences.

Another definition, endorsed more frequently by women in general, is that intimacy is the profound risk of vulnerability before another that allows for love; in Maslow's terms, this is "to be deeply understood and deeply accepted."[2] This perspective acknowledges sex as a potential part of intimacy, but never the totality of it. It defines intimacy as a voluntary, mutual sharing — a self-disclosure — of what is most essential within, an exposing of inner thoughts, secrets, and values to the scrutiny of another in the expectation of understanding and acceptance *and* the assumption that the other will reciprocate. The risks are tremendous: potential ridicule, rejection, violation of confidentiality, or lack of reciprocity, to name a few. The benefits are also tremendous: deepened understanding, greater love, improved communication, profound mutuality. To appreciate intimacy in this sense, four key words must be stressed: self-disclosing, free, mutual, and energizing.

The self-disclosing aspect of intimacy demands self-revelation involving values, both public and private, and feelings. More than reporting events or opinions about events, it is the riskier business of exposing the deeper part of myself — how I feel about events and why. Self-disclosure is impossible without communication; therefore, forcing another to guess my likes and dislikes through observing my behavior is insufficient. Betty Berzon says in her book *Permanent Partners:*

> Good communication is the pathway to intimacy in a relationship. To allow another person access to your inner reality, to the hopes, the dreams, the fears, and the doubts that motivate your life is to make the most intimate kind of contact with another. It is what distinguishes love from infatuation and real partnership from romantic illusion.[3]

Self-disclosure must be freely offered, not demanded. To insist that I tell you my secrets does not make me intimate with you. Freedom to self-disclose is obviously rooted in trust, the expectation that you will accept what I offer in the same sacred mode in which I present it. Self-disclosure in and of itself is not intimate if it is coerced.

Mutuality is the flow of intimacy, the back-and-forth reciprocity and respect generated when two people trust themselves to one another. One-way self-disclosures are not intimate relationships. For example, it is common for persons in counseling or spiritual direction to believe they are in love with their counselors or directors precisely because they have revealed so much to their helpers. The resulting vulnerability and trust in risk-taking delude some counselees and directees into a feeling of intimacy that does not really exist because the self-disclosure is not mutual.

Finally, intimacy must be energizing, embracing that "special elusive feeling" of uniqueness, life, and exclusivity that sets what we share together apart from what we share with others in our lives. Some refer to it as chemistry; others call it a sixth sense. Bernard Shaw could have been speaking to this aspect of intimacy when he wrote, "Love is a gross exaggeration of the difference between one person and everybody else."

For the most part, men in our culture have been conditioned to be independent and autonomous and, subsequently, to avoid vulnerability. Intimacy as self-disclosure is threatening to many because it demands a melting of the armor of self-sufficiency and an active engagement in the "stuff" of relationship, feelings, and emotions. Women religious who went through pre–Vatican II formation were steeped in this male model view so that they, like men, could be "above" emotional involvements and the vicissitudes of interpersonal interactions.

For these reasons, then, Levinson found that men did not have best friends;[4] for the same reasons, vowed celibates were not supposed to have best friends. A best friend, one who knows all about me and loves me anyway, is too threatening to the complete Western male — and vowed celibate — bent on the culturally and ecclesiastically prescribed project of independence and autonomy.

It seems that many vowed celibates simply refuse to comply with cultural conditioning and early formation training when it comes to intimacy in their lives; 97 percent of the women and 89 percent of the men who responded to my questionnaire reported having a best friend. Like women in general, the overwhelming majority of sisters named another woman, generally another woman religious, as their best friend. Unlike men in general, who, if they claim a best friend, name a woman, the majority of brothers and priests, 59 percent of them, named another man as best friend. Most vowed celibates readily acknowledge that they would not be where they are today, personally, ministerially, or spiritually, were it not for their relationships. As one 43-year-old order priest wrote:

> Intimacy is most important to me — I'm not alone — someone knows me and loves me with no string attached. It is the greatest source of growth I've ever had. [It] has forced me to face blind spots, prejudice, buried pain and gives a sense of joy and meaning to life itself. Friendship has been the keystone of growth in my life. Because of it I am a much more effective priest — more open, more warm, more compassionate, more responsive, understanding, etc. It has been the greatest source of support in my life in dealing with stress — someone to turn to where I can be most completely myself. . . . It's a dangerous road, friendship is, in terms of sexuality, but it certainly is far more dangerous to repress sexuality than to find legitimate forms of expression. I firmly believe we cannot love God more than we love the human being that we're closest to on earth.

Along the same lines, a 48-year-old sister wrote, "I have been able to see aspects of my personality which I would have never discovered alone. My friends have shown me the humanity of Jesus and helped me appreciate the dignity of person."

Middle-aged priests and religious, as part of their training, were exhorted to develop detachment in their relationships, to leave both place and person behind following transfer to new sites and local communities. This is another early mandate that did not "take," since over half the respondents indicated that their primary relationship had been going on for ten years or longer and was maintained through letters, phone calls, or visits on at least a monthly, if not more frequent, basis. This is common among women in general, but not among men in general. The mobile lifestyle of today's ministry does impose challenge, as this order priest, age 52, explained:

> I'm "rootless" — apt to be transferred to another state. Going from frequent get-togethers to a weekly or monthly phone call or letter — this hurts. With one or two delightful exceptions, the relationship has cooled down or even died. Friendship has always been at the top of the heap for

me.... As an adult I find myself with about four or five really close friends with whom I share just about everything. Of these, two know me as I really and fully am — dark corners as well as bright spots. What a joy and support these two guys are! I am the same for them. Often, however, I've been disappointed in friendship. I've been transferred; some of my friends are no longer friends — just friendly acquaintances.

That vowed celibates tend to name other vowed celibates as best friends is probably a function of shared values and proximity. Commitment to ministry, lived faith stance, interest in Church, and belief in prayer are values commonly endorsed by priests and men and women religious; it seems only logical that ministers will be attracted to others who share and want to discuss them. Proximity, living with or close to another, is undoubtedly why so many vowed celibates are best friends with one another. This seems more true for women than men, because over half the women religious, while only 27 percent of the men, named another member of their own congregation as best friend. Historically, women religious had less mobility than vowed men, which may explain why so many more of the women name a best friend intracongregationally.

While most relational gender differences reported for women and men in general do not appear applicable to vowed celibates conditioned to the male model, some do. Naming a woman as best friend significantly increases the belief of being named best friend in return. Having a female best friend also significantly increases the likelihood of hearing "I love you" and of shedding and seeing tears. Finally, having a female best friend significantly increases the expectation that she will contact you if she has either good or bad news.[5] Worded negatively, those who name a male as best friend are less likely to assume mutuality of friendship, to hear "I love you," to see or shed tears, or to be contacted in an emergency, either positive or negative. This suggests that some aspects of the strong, silent male stereotype exist within the intimacies of vowed celibates.

Gender was not a significant variable in other emotional expressions between friends. Vowed celibates report that they can tell when their friend is happy, angry, sad, upset, or distressed, and that their best friend can read these same emotions in return.

Many of the items for the questionnaire were derived from

material in the psychology of women, especially Schaef, and the extensive study by Michael McGill, *The McGill Report: On Male Intimacy.*[6] McGill distributed an Intimacy Questionnaire to 1,383 people (737 men and 646 women) between the ages of 18 and 73, followed by in-depth interviews with 70 men, 70 women, and 20 couples. Intrinsic to his investigation was his definition of intimacy as level of self-disclosure rather than genital involvement.

Like other behavioral scientists in the field, McGill found that the men in his study did not have best friends. If they did name another, it was generally a woman. In those instances where respondents named another man, McGill pursued them with phone calls, only to discover that the so-called best friend was stunned to learn that he had been named and/or that the two men had not been in contact for years. Clearly, celibate men and women religious trained into the male model do not parallel McGill's findings.

McGill discovered that most men withhold themselves from their wives; fewer than 10 percent had been fully disclosing with their spouses in every arena. The majority, over 65 percent, were partially disclosing while nearly 25 percent disclosed very little.

"Well," some may conclude, "what do you expect? If men don't know how to disclose, then they don't know how to disclose!" Not true, says McGill. He found that a significant majority of the men he investigated regularly disclosed to another woman — but not the spouse. The "other woman" might be a relative, co-worker, or neighbor, but *not* a sexual partner; once the relationship became an "affair," the men ceased to self-disclose. Another finding: Men would self-disclose to the woman without reciprocating listening and nurturing. The other woman was a "relational fix" who did not judge or interfere with his life. Stuart Miller discussed the same phenomenon in his book *Men and Friendship.*[7] He claimed that rugged individualism and competitiveness among men militate against male intimacy. Many, he found, "used" women as emotional support systems, but frequently ended up boring them because they contributed so little input of their own male persons to the intimacy exchange.

Celibate men, and women religious trained to emulate the male model, do not "fit" these findings either. First of all, they report enjoying intimate relationships. Second, over half the men name another man as best friend. Third, both the women and men feel they know everything about them. Fourth, more than 80 percent of the vowed celibates indicate enjoying mutual and full self-disclosure in their intimate relationships at least 50 percent or more of the time. Fifth, vowed celibates claim to share talk time equally, to listen carefully and to be heard well, and to be appreciative of and appreciated by the best friend. Sixth, vowed celibates do not compete in their relationships (a male model trait), but work through differences until they reach some level of mutually satisfying resolution — not necessarily agreement. A diocesan priest explained:

> It is extremely important for me that, while we may disagree and sometimes disagree rather extensively, a good/best friend will continue to respect the differences and not allow them to determine our relationship because it is based on healthy respect for each other, including our differences. It is my view that any good relationship must contain not only similar values and beliefs but also a deep respect for what is different and challenging. When one thinks they know the other completely, then the relationship is doomed. Surprises are vital to deepening any relationship and to allowing growth in both persons. (AGE 49)

Through his extensive research, McGill teased out five elements of intimacy in which men and women differ: time, variety, depth, exclusivity, and "we-ness." In all, vowed celibates are more similar to women than men.

For women, time is freeing; for men, limiting. Women share time together and perceive it as a gift allowing them to catch up on each other. Men, more time bound, prefer to talk about what they have shared together in the past, such as school or work, but seldom fill the gaps of their lives while they were apart. Subsequently, women anticipate time together to recount events, feelings, and reactions since their last gathering; men frequently dread what they see as a boring burden of rehashing what they have been through before. It is hypothesized that men are reluctant to discuss experiences not shared within a specific time frame with another because of introducing new and potentially vulnerable material. It is as if the man says to himself, "I know what happened when we were in school together and I know how they felt about what I did then.

I'm not so sure of how they'll react to my latest business deal or to my decisions with my family, so I'll keep the conversation safe." This may explain why so many men fail to keep up with people they know once they change jobs or move.

Vowed celibates do not reflect the male model attitude toward time in their relationships. Eighty-five percent of celibate women and men report that their discussions focus primarily on their current lives rather than on past shared experiences. They work to keep their relationships current, even when separated by great distances. The pain of this was expressed by one man:

> The most difficult part is that I always know that some day I will have to leave. It is especially difficult when my friend refuses to admit that that is a possibility. It makes it difficult to start new relationships as well as continue present relationships when the time comes to move on. Right now, I am beginning my third year in my present assignment. My best friends are all a thousand miles away, literally. It is great when we get together, which happens about once or twice a year. It is hard to remain close over the phone, but still we work at it. . . . Each time I move, it seems to take longer to establish a close local friend. Many people seem to believe that priests don't need friends, or that other priests are their close friends. It's not true, at least not for me. When I move on, at first I miss my friends, in a sort of selfish way. But as we keep in contact and get together for vacations, we seem to enter a new — sometimes even closer — relationship because we cherish the times we spend together. (ORDER PRIEST, AGE 35)

McGill's second element of intimacy, variety, is treasured and exercised more by women than men. He found that while women are comfortable discussing many different topics with one another, men tend to restrict themselves to tried-and-true shared experiences such as hunting trips, school days, and athletic events. We used to have a standing joke at my college pertaining to this. We noticed that when women gathered in the faculty room, we expected them to discuss just about anything; when men gathered, we predicted they would talk about sex, sports, or money. It is safer for male model (Schaef uses the term male system) persons to restrict conversations to things and events because then they can exert more control; they are less vulnerable talking about things than personal reactions or feelings.

Vowed celibates indicate that variety is very important to them in their relationships. They discuss so many different things with their significant other that they believe they could write the friend's biography, and vice versa. They talk about work, play, and prayer; they know where their best friend stands financially and sexually (two topics verboten to the men in McGill's study) and believe the friend knows the same about them. However, they are not overly dependent because they feel free to pursue hobbies and activities with others as well. Of course, not every vowed celibate enjoys this perfect balance. For example:

> Our friendship has gone through numerous phases. I stepped back when another entered her life. She tells me that this friendship is different from ours, and I believe her. At the same time, I find her choosing vacations with this other friend instead of with me. I have come to expect this, so I do not fret it. I also have other friends. We are both strong personalities and when we see things differently, it is time for volatility. Yet our friendship continues. We try to get together when we are in the same city. We support each other in difficult times and in great joy. (SISTER, AGE 57)

Depth, McGill's third element of intimacy, refers to the level of self-disclosure in a conversation. In this, women display more depth more often than do men. Public information, such as favorite foods or clothes or location of work, is the least revealing and the most often employed by men. Men's conversations, in general, focus on things and events rather than on personal reactions to them. McGill recounts the story of one man's shock upon discovering that his so-called best friend, a hunting buddy, committed suicide. He had no idea that his best friend suffered from marital tension, financial difficulty, and general depression, and McGill wondered how it was possible to have a best friend about whom one knew so little. Women, on the other hand, demonstrate considerably more depth in their interpersonal interactions, even though they are frequently criticized for being "too emotional" or for "personalizing" too much.

Celibate women and men enjoy extensive depth of sharing with their best friend. They report mutually satisfying conversations on faith, prayer, and philosophy of life. A 45-year-old brother wrote:

> The amount of sharing at feeling level — it *can* be done if there is an openness, honesty, willingness to listen, and willingness to self-disclose. How wonderful people can really be — at their best — the intimacy that can be mutually experienced — trust, sensitivity, openness, caring. Often many people become "busy about many things" — and *time* and *distance* often, I find, allows a person (some) to let go of the relationship/friendship. Some people fear revealing themselves — and sometimes fear intimacy and self-disclosure; this saddens me. Many people desire to be *listened to* but often do not know *how* to listen. Friendships are important to me. I see great value in being able to love, affirm, support, care for another/others and experience this returned when it comes. I strongly feel that friendship, as of any love, must be *freely given*, it cannot be forced, manipulated, choreographed, demanded. I feel it must be worked at if both parties desire it, but it cannot be received/given unless done so in freedom. *Mutuality* is important. Sadly, at times, I find people very desirous to be *listened to* but often enough, they themselves do not *listen* well. *Listening to another* in a friendship or a love relationship is *essential* for its growth — how else can we come to know, understand, love one another? Sometimes time and distance can erode contact/communication — friendship can die for lack of nurturing. This saddens me above all when it happens. It takes *two* people to work at it over *time* and *distance*, and yet, the "fading away" of friendship must be eventually accepted and respected. Nevertheless, losing someone I care for is, for me, a great sadness." (emphasis his)

Exclusivity, McGill's fourth intimacy element, refers to the uniqueness of each relationship, the "specialness" between two people that is unlike anything they share with anyone else. Stuart Miller could have been writing about this when he noted that each "relationship is its own context." Women, for example, know that playing tennis with person x is very different from playing tennis with person y, not just because of skill level difference, but more importantly, because of personality differences; the tennis outing is

qualitatively different, depending on the partner involved. Therefore, many women agree to events more for the people involved
than for the events themselves and may cancel their plans when
the personality complexion of participants changes. McGill's men
were very different in this regard; they tended to view people as
"interchangeable parts" with whom they pursued events, so if one
person was unable to go, they simply called another. Worded another way: for women, friends make the event; for men, events
make the friend.

In reporting their intimacies, vowed celibates seem more like
the women than the men in McGill's study. They feel that their
relationship with their best friend is very special, and even though
their early training insisted they give up past relationships for the
sake of present assignment, they do not live that way. An order
priest, 39 years old, wrote:

> I've changed rather radically in my approach [to friendship]
> in the last five years because of my love and care for my best
> friend _____. Before, I had a long list of friends — I am
> popular and a good person — I was often chosen. I would do
> many things with many people — going for breadth rather
> than depth. This was more "acceptable," no great fears about
> remaining celibate, etc. It was very ego gratifying for me. It
> was easy. I didn't have to grow or change or own my feelings
> or be very responsible. I was a social butterfly. Now, because
> I am faithful to my friend, I see I've grown in commitment
> and dedication. I've more and more faced my weakness. I am
> more alive, more real, more happy.

Of course, many vowed celibates acknowledge how difficult it
is to maintain a specialness within their relationships because of
changing ministries and living situations. A sister explained it this
way:

> The transitory nature of our life is a problem. Appointments
> that move us out of state so often with little chance of contact
> then except for a few brief encounters during the summer.
> Hard to sustain a deep friendship that way! The heart cries
> for some sort of stability in relationships, yet keeps getting
> uprooted. This has been the #1 reason why people I *have*

been close to have become less so over the passage of time.
(AGE 40)

A cleric in his mid-forties wrote that he was perceived by many as "a great friend," but deep inside felt he was no one's friend. His struggle was to risk relationship that was truly mutual — a big departure from his earlier (and safer) one-sided giving. A 48-year-old diocesan priest explained his relational growth:

> Friendship is a value I've struggled to learn. The need for friendship has grown as I age. Some of my relationships I've hurt or destroyed due to lack of "know how" on my part. In some relationships, people have asked for more than I could give.

McGill identified "we-ness" as the fifth element of intimacy, which is described as the extent of mutuality (or lack of it) in decision making. He found that males in his study often said "we" when they really meant "me," whereas females generally meant it when they said "we." While McGill's men frequently made decisions for themselves and their partners without consulting the partner, women seldom did.

Vowed celibates report high levels of mutuality in their intimate relationships when initiating and terminating conversation and visits, planning vacations, and sharing values, ideas, and philosophies. They actively schedule private time together to catch up on their lives and, frequently, to pray together. When one person's ministerial demands or geographical distance impose boundaries on the time the two can spend together, *both* partners negotiate the limits.

What many vowed celibates seem to be saying is that intimacy, characterized by meaningful conversation and high levels of self-disclosure and mutuality, is very important to them. Eschewing early training proscribing close relationship, celibate men and women are claiming and living intimate involvement. This is not always easy, and some find their early training in both culture and Church difficult to overcome. For example:

> I was always afraid of developing an intimate relationship with someone. I think I thought it'd automatically become

genital. I've discovered this doesn't have to happen like it does in the movies. Now that I've pursued intimacy, I wish I would have done it earlier. It would have helped my growth as a human. [I regret] that I was "hung up" re: past relationships and didn't trust myself or others to be sexual, intimate *and* celibate. (ORDER CLERIC, AGE 49)

Literature in adult development suggests that the capacity to be intimate increases with age and experience, a finding that holds for vowed celibates as well; no one blossoms into middle age somehow magically, relationally competent. It's a growth process, as described by this 40-year-old sister:

I notice my twenties were characterized by short, intense relationships — usually lasting around two years — I loved the excitement and intensity of new relationships. As I experienced my thirties I found I had more staying power. Several of the friendships I have now are 8–10 years old and are strong enough to last forever. I definitely see a connection with maturity and recovery — getting in touch with co-dependency and COA issues has definitely changed my ability for intimacy.

Another sister, age 52, wrote at length about her journey in friendship:

I am learning that many of my past friends used me as a listener and I was not getting my needs met. I am learning how to be mutual in relationships and also to pick people as friends selectively — not indiscriminately nor ones that need lots of help. Current relationships: I find it takes energy and time to have a good relationship, and so I must go slow and let the friendship evolve gradually. It costs. Past friendships: I looked for friends who filled a *need* in me and know now that only I can nurture myself with God's help. I've had a difficult time with friendships these past ten years. Some close friends (three of them) in community have left, another is at a great distance. I've also had major family losses. I have flailed around trying to find my way. Two other friends in community share the same sense. I experience, as do they, more aloneness and loneliness than ever. I have more good close friends out of community now than in community. I have to trust what's happening, yet periodically I get a twinge of conscience about "a good sister *should* have her closest friends in community." It just doesn't work that way anymore, especially for those of us who have branched out into more diverse ministries.

Growth in relational skills assumes much stretching and plenty of mistakes. Several people told me they'd suffered a number of "intimacy disasters" because of too much independence or dependence, because of control issues, lack of boundaries, or mistrust rooted in dysfunctional family histories. Some had succumbed to fear or peer pressure when they would have preferred to follow their hearts. Many, like this 54-year-old sister, had to learn to adjust to personality differences:

[What I find most important about relationships] besides the exquisite joy of feeling safe, accepted and reverenced by another — the graces of self-revelation — the asceticism of mutual growth. My natural propensity for privacy — for space — is at times "invaded" by the requirements of the friending. Sometimes I want to hide — to avoid an intensity that is present. My friendships have been gifts for me. They have at the same time caused me the greatest anxieties and stretchings and the most joy. The "significant other" relationship is a place of safety and growth — and very much integral to my being in God.

A common theme of many write-in comments was the sense of freedom and fullness experienced through relationship. Many — more women than men — said that personal intimacies, with all the joys and sorrows involved, brought them to deeper closeness with God (one sister wrote that a true best friend was "God with skin on"), a more profound appreciation of life, and a richer depth of prayer. The obstacle to intimacy most frequently mentioned by both women and men was the "busy-ness" of their lives, which could, if they allowed it, take precedence over quality time with the friend. No one reported completely smooth relational development; several felt they had been "used" more than once. The importance of communication was stressed by most respondents and articulated well by this sister, 49 years old:

> Friendship is a mutual gift each gives the other freely. It cannot be forced or hurried. Fidelity is a great blessing of a true relationship. Also, God must be present, so the focus on each other is not all-absorbing. The ability to talk about real issues is significant, I believe. This focus keeps perspective in the relationship. You are changed and influenced by your friendships — and so is your friend. To be conscious of "being yourself," while yet bringing your "best self" to the relationship, is important. If you are open, your friend helps *bring out* your best self and vice versa. Sometimes you need to talk about expectations in your friendship — hurts and disappointments, troubles, fears, hopes. These reveal more of "who you are" and are risks, but are necessary ones to entrust to your friend's ear or confidence. They are the core "stuff" of a really wholesome and lasting relationship/ bond.

Some vowed celibates talked with me personally about their experiences with the friendship questions. Two women religious in their late thirties who had been friends since formation told me how affirming it was for both of them to complete the items together, reminding the other that she was, in fact, the best friend. A diocesan priest in his early fifties related what a great time he had just thinking about his best friend while working through the items. A sister, 37 years old, found the questionnaire painful because it highlighted for her how really distant she was from the one she called friend and how one-sided the relationship had become. For her, it precipitated some serious evaluating of the role and value of the relationship in her life and raised the question of her willingness to drop the relationship, to maintain the status quo even though it was unsatisfying, or to push for a new level of intimacy. A 41-year-old diocesan priest recounted how the items stirred memories of his best friend:

> I met Joe sixteen years ago as a newly ordained. He was ten years older. Our friendship grew, and because his teaching took him to _____, our "get-togethers" were regular — on

the phone and as often as possible in person. In January 1988, I came back from a ski vacation to be told by a seminarian (who did not know Joe was my best friend) that "some priest" had died and would be buried in two days. He couldn't remember the last name — when he did, I almost dropped in the hall. The funeral was traumatic. I think I cried for a week. I called the priest who had introduced us sixteen years earlier and "just let it out." Some weeks later, he and I had a dinner in honor of Joe — we laughed and cried. That broke the depression. I still miss Joe. I'll probably never have a priest friend of that depth and type again.

Truly a sad story. Thank God this man had another in whom he could confide his feelings for Joe, in whom he could entrust his delight and grief. Too often, in counseling, at workshops, and through the questionnaire, I heard laments over the subterfuge, the conspiracy of silence, surrounding intimacy among celibates. Many do not feel free to talk about this aspect of their lives, especially with other celibates, for fear of censure or scandal. Assuming they will be judged harshly, they prefer to share little or nothing of one of the greatest delights of their life — intimacy. In fact, last summer at Notre Dame, two men religious — best friends — who had completed the questionnaire asked if we could have lunch together. They wanted to know what I had learned from all the other respondents to see if they were alone in their experience: Were they the only ones to feel so strongly for another? Were they the only ones who felt pressure to "keep quiet" about their intimacy? "If we're all going through this in one way or another," concluded one of them, "then it can only help us to talk about it."

In summary, men and women religious and diocesan clerics, in general, believe in and cultivate intimate friendships. Valuing their friends, they delight in the mutuality of personal exchange and quality time together and believe themselves to be better persons for taking the risks involved. Overall, it seems that celibate males do not fit the relational stereotypes of men in general, nor do celibate women and men live out the scripts of detachment and isolation promulgated during early formation. Men and women both acknowledge a strong spiritual dimension to their relationships, noting a correlation between growth in human intimacy and growth in God-relating. Most exciting, many vowed celibates seem willing to stay with the process, ambiguity and all, in their quest for relational authenticity.

Chapter 3

SEXUAL, CELIBATE, OR SEXUAL CELIBATE?

Up to this past year I have not told another person about my sexual involvements and no celibate person has told me their story. Because of my ministry, people have shared with me their infidelities or struggles with sexuality, mostly homosexuality. Within community, our discussions about spirituality are exclusive of sexuality and I think we all assume we are all living celibate, nongenital lives — and the big secret exists between me and people I'm involved with. When I was in formation (which was about eight years), every one of my significant relationships was questioned by a superior at one point or another. My responses were mostly defensive, yet I continued to live my friendships the way I thought was meaningful and responsive. After vows, I've never been questioned. And I think if you would ask most people in my community who my friends are, they could name the top three. . . . I still move in and out of having guilt about it [genital expression] and find myself in fluctuation about the compatibility of celibate life and sexual involvement. On my best days, I am aware that I am not fully what I want to be in any of my vows — along with them, celibacy is more goal than reality. (SISTER, AGE 40)

The term "sexual involvements" can include many actions. I am looking at it as a freedom to be affectionate — hug, hold hands, kiss — not genital intercourse. I choose celibacy freely — believe it makes me available for ministry and for different people — can love many. Friends have been a great help for loneliness. (ORDER PRIEST, AGE 60)

The [sexual] experiences have been a rich source of self-discovery and learning about friendships and discovering my body, as well as my spirit. I think an attitude of guilt kills the spirit and spoils the soul. I can only know that a sexual encounter in the context of relationship of mutual love and care has been/is a gift — but one that I must handle with discretion. The vow of celibacy is not just about lack of sexual activity — it is an "attitude of the heart." It is a right spirit — a way of living, of using my body, my sexuality, and my spirit for the sake of God's kingdom. It is a gift that is given to *some* people. It need not be a requirement for ministry or for community. *And*, a sexual encounter in the context of a loving, life-giving relationship does not necessarily mean that I'm not being faithful to my vow. However, if the sexual expression (meaning intercourse or genital sexual expression) becomes a priority, I would need to re-evaluate my desire to live as a celibate. (SISTER, AGE 40)

One of the things I've learned is that we grow into the vows. Somehow I had convinced myself that I didn't have to worry about being unfaithful since I had vowed chastity. Naive — yes. I am a perfectionist and so things were pretty black and white. I have learned better what it means to have inner authority and to exercise it. I never expected to fail in a sexual way. I forgot that I was an incomplete and very human being. I was caught off guard both interiorly and externally. (SISTER, AGE 52)

Celibacy is a *process* of growth, not a state of being. To grow means to take risks, and sometimes to make mistakes. But it also means to continue to search for the way to be most loving, most fully human within the context of a commitment. I have never had intercourse with any of my friends. However, the sharing of intimate affection, including sleeping together naked, has been a deeply bonding and meaningful manifestation of the love that we share. I struggle sometimes with questions of appropriateness in relation to our commitments, and with some guilt. Yet, I find the sharing to be a very freeing, healing, and enlivening part of my life. My self-confidence has been strengthened, and my relational skills in ministry have been sharpened. I am grateful for the gift of these relationships, and for the direction, challenge, and life they give to my life as man, as priest, as minister. (DIOCESAN PRIEST, AGE 46)

Sexuality is a fascinating and fearsome expression of humanity that can be a freeing and life-giving manifestation of affection or a crippling and cruel impediment to intimacy, depending upon how the individual defines the term. Sexuality is shrouded in ambiguity due to the legacy of centuries of repression and fear, both socially and ecclesiastically, and contemporary vowed celibates are, like their lay sisters and brothers, confused about the role of sexuality in their lives. Just what does it mean to be sexual? Can I be sexual and celibate, and if so, how? What is the most authentic way for me to be intimate and faithful to my commitments at the same time?

There are no easy answers to these questions, but some realities, based on my experiences with religious as well as on findings from my research, exist: (1) vowed celibates are struggling with the questions; (2) significant numbers of vowed celibates report themselves to be sexually active; (3) many vowed celibates believe they can be intimate, sexual, and celibate; (4) many vowed celibates feel that sexuality and celibacy are processes rather than products; (5) vowed celibates who have been or are sexually active may report regret or guilt about their behaviors, but feel that their experiences have challenged them to greater depths of personal and spiritual growth and, therefore, report that they are better persons as a result; (6) there are no universally accepted definitions of sexuality and celibacy among middle-aged vowed celibates today.

This does not mean that all is quiet and peaceful on the sexually celibate front. On the contrary, many vowed celibates suffer the tyranny of sexual fear and repression, sexual addictions, addiction and co-dependency issues that facilitate sex while mitigating against sexuality, adult survivor issues, and sexual orientation questions. Several wonder why they should even bother with the questions. "After all," they reason, "life was much simpler when we didn't talk about sex and celibacy was clearly defined as no friends, no affection, no sex." In all of my counseling and workshop contacts, I have yet to meet someone who is totally free of sexual "hang ups," regardless of how well integrated she or he seems to be.

The Legacy

Confusion surrounding sexuality and celibacy is rooted in a long history of cultural and ecclesial repression and misunderstanding that continues to influence contemporary thought.[1] A complete review is beyond the scope of this discussion, but a few salient points might provide a backdrop for understanding today's dilemmas.

Western thought, with its emphasis on dualisms, differentiated between the spiritual and material, relegating the material to lower and, subsequently, more sinful status. As the Church struggled to define the virtues of celibacy and chastity, sex, even within marriage, was viewed as "less holy" than celibate abstinence; the truly elect, the saved, the holy would not "lower" themselves to engage in such carnal pursuits. Married people themselves were urged to abstain from intercourse on the day prior to receiving communion and later were encouraged to refrain from intercourse on other days as well for other religious reasons: abstinence on Wednesday in honor of Ash Wednesday, on Thursday in memory of Holy Thursday, on Friday because of Good Friday, on Saturday in honor of the Blessed Virgin Mary, on Sunday out of respect for the Resurrection, and on Monday in reparation for the Poor Souls.[2]

To better understand and control carnal behaviors, civil and Church authorities developed detailed lists of specific genital behaviors and determined which were acceptable and which were not. Heterosexual intercourse in the missionary position for purposes of procreation was allowed; other physical expressions for other purposes were viewed as suspect if not actually illegal or sinful.[3]

An extreme example of sexual repression and its concomitant preoccupation is the Victorian era, which profoundly impacted contemporary mentality about sex and sexuality, since so much of early U.S. and Canadian culture was developed by individuals steeped in its legacy. In its prim and proper exterior, Victorianism affected a façade of humans who were pure, lofty, and in control of their passions, untouched by and disinterested in carnal pursuits. Tables and pianos were draped in crocheted "skirts" so that people would not be distracted by "legs" during concerts and social visits. Women's copious hooped skirts were designed to project asexuality, and some people went so far as to suggest that men wear skirts so their genitals would not be rubbed and aroused by tight-fitting trousers. Classic texts suggesting genital behavior or even sexual allusions were expurgated. Thomas Bowdler, a nineteenth-century editor, rewrote both Shakespeare and the Bible, eliminating any passages of overt or covert sensuality. The term "bowdlerize" came to mean the eliminating or expurgating of that which is vulgar. Needless to say, in light of such extreme repression, a rich and lucrative underworld of pornography and prostitution flourished.

The medical profession contributed little to rectify the situation. Products of their culture, physicians during the 1800s believed that too much sexual activity ("too much" was never defined) led to a host of physical and psychological ills and generally relied on folklore rooted in fear and misinformation when consulted by patients about genital issues. That no one in the medical community saw human sexual response as a legitimate area of study until the middle of the twentieth century is itself quite telling. When Dr. William Masters published his initial findings, he was treated as a pariah by other physicians. By his own account, he was accused of being disgusting and unprofessional in his pursuit of such an area of investigation.

Academicians were also silent. When Alfred Kinsey published his report on male sexual behavior in 1948 and on female sexual behavior in 1953, both extensive survey studies, he was called before the House Un-American Activities Committee and accused of being a communist.[4] This might explain why no comparable research projects were undertaken for the next twenty years.

Today's Reality

By the time today's middle-aged population was going through childhood and adolescence, both Church and sociocultural structures were quite repressive and negative about sex, sexuality, and affectivity. Narrow definitions of appropriate behaviors spawned fear and suspicion that, in turn, created enormous amounts of curiosity and ambivalence. To protect themselves from either sin or social disgrace, young people were advised to avoid all and any situations that could possibly lead to genital involvement. They were alienated from touch because it might lead to hugging; they dared not hug because they might become sexually aroused; they must never become sexually aroused because they might... and on and on. Somewhere in this negative reductionistic reasoning, people learned to divorce their sex from their sexuality. In other words, they saw their genital behaviors as somehow removed from the larger picture of themselves as male or female persons.

Don Goergen explains this well in *The Sexual Celibate* as he clearly outlines the differences among sexuality, affectivity, and genitality. Sexuality, he maintains, is the totality of each of us as persons, including our gender assignment (being male or female), our feelings, thoughts, relationships, and work. Everything we do is sexual because we do everything as women or men. Eating a meal, running in the park, being attracted to women or men — all of these are sexual behaviors integrally tied up with our understandings of ourselves as enfleshed beings, female or male. In this, Goergen asserts, all people are called to be sexual and to develop actively their sexuality. Most people do not define sexuality as Goergen does; instead, they equate sexual with genital or with being heterosexual or homosexual/lesbian. True, genitality and sexual orientation are *part* of being sexual, but they tell very little about the total sexuality of an individual.

Affection is the good, necessary, and pleasant reaching out to another that conveys so much of what we feel for the other. Communicated through posture, tone, looks, and touch, affection is essential for all humans. Psychologists have established that babies die from lack of it; we don't know yet how many adults do. Goergen acknowledges that most people in our culture are starved for affection.

Goergen's third dimension, genitality, refers specifically to genital behaviors — all of them. Too often, people fall into the legalistic rationalization that only heterosexual genital intercourse (preferably in the missionary position) "counts" as real sex. Oral sex, anal sex, and mutual masturbation are explained away as less real or less serious than the "real thing." Thus, many of today's middle-aged population grew up believing that it was okay to "mess around," just so they didn't go "all the way." Such rationalization becomes possible when people learn to divorce sex from sexuality and develop, as a result, very mechanistic understandings of what "counts" and what doesn't. It is consistent with the male system belief that intimacy equals sex and, subsequently, sex equals intercourse.

Goergen's message is both simple and profound: Celibates are expected to be sexual, affectional, and nongenital, even though they might make "genital mistakes" in learning about their sexual and affectionate selves. Goergen's challenge is more difficult than it seems, because vowed celibates, like all women and men who grew up during the middle of the twentieth century, had little or no experience with positive intimacy, affection, and sexuality.

Today's middle-aged adults learned to fear affection and sexuality because they grew up during the era of silence and repression surrounding sex and intimacy. They know well what it was like to sit expectantly as youngsters in hushed classrooms and retreat conferences while teachers and priests warned them about "sins against the sixth and ninth commandments," yearning to hear and learn more while fearing to express too much interest or ignorance. In many cases, they received very little sex education per se, and what little they had was too frequently presented as academic, sterile, and distant from any integration with relationships and love. Boys tended to hear lots about masturbation and its consequences; girls tended to hear much about menstruation and their role as sexual moral guardians. Neither tended to hear much at all about sex, love, and relationship. Partial information and misinformation were rampant as many young people learned half the story from their friends who had, at best, a quarter of the plot.

Pre–Vatican II formation programs, in general, provided little, if any, antidote to the culture's cloak of guilt and silence. Young women and men, often naive about the fundamentals of human sexual response and reproduction, entered novitiates and seminaries where sex, affection, and relationships were seldom discussed except in proscriptive terms. Preparation for vowed life often consisted of lengthy treatment of poverty and obedience lasting many months and including numerous readings, while coverage of chastity was limited to a single lecture or, in one case, a single sheet of paper passed in a sealed envelope from novice to novice. Novices and seminarians learned what *not* to do, but received little on the positive side of the ledger about what to do (besides repress) to live and love genuinely. (In fairness to formation personnel of that era, we should note that little substantive material on healthy relational development was available to pass on.)

As these women and men graduated from their formation programs and moved into formal ministry, they encountered two experiences for which they were totally unprepared: (1) the sexual revolution and (2) the challenges of adult development, especially the upheaval of midlife transition.

The sexual revolution celebrated sex in song and deed and claimed that freedom from sexual hang-ups was the answer to all society's ills. To abandon sexual repression, fear, and guilt, the revolution's proponents proclaimed, was to free oneself to unity and harmony with the self and with others. The unquestioned, insidious underlying assumption was the simplistic belief that pleasurable, uninhibited sex would, in and of itself, *create* intimate, meaningful, and lasting relationships. Good sex would lead to instant intimacy; good sex would alleviate loneliness; good sex would eradicate interpersonal tensions. Such a philosophy was enormously seductive to a culture steeped in centuries of ecclesiastical and social sexual repression that had, unwittingly, through its very repression, created barely contained sexual interest and energy — often far out of proportion to what was warranted, given that sex is one aspect among many in the human endeavor.

While trying to make sense out of the cultural flip-flop from sexual repression to sexual abandon, newly emerging ministers found that adulthood was not as predictable as they had been led to believe it would be. They found themselves challenged professionally, morally, and interpersonally; they discovered that the old answers did not always work for the new questions. In short, they learned that, contrary to their earlier expectations, life does not get easier with age. They learned that external rules and forms must give way to inner conviction and self-sustaining identities rooted in personal authenticity.

Vowed Celibates and Sexuality Today

How are vowed celibates today, especially those who grew up in a pre–Vatican II Church and now live in a post–Vatican II middle age, defining sexuality and its role in their lives? How are they reconciling their early formation training with their lived reality as growing, loving, and learning adults?

Today's middle-aged celibates seem to have rejected the "hands off" proscriptions of their formation training to enjoy affection in their lives. Many report the importance of warm, close, affectionate expressions and how vital these are to their personal and interpersonal connectedness. A 40-year-old sister explained her experience:

> For more than twenty years, I struggled with the pain of living in a "hands-off" environment. A "hearty handshake" was the only "official" greeting. Thank God we've become a far warmer and more expressive community of women. But such deprivation runs havoc in one's psyche — the more one doesn't have even the barest minimum, the greater the craving. The entire year after my father died, I would have given anything to have simply been held by someone.

An ongoing struggle for many is to determine how they can be appropriately affectionate without becoming inappropriately genital. Most work this out over time as they experiment within relationships. A 45-year-old brother wrote:

> As a teenager I had no dating experience, so my friendship over these years has been a beautiful growth experience in learning about true friendship, experiencing real intimacy through sharing and some physical contact that did not involve intercourse at any time. As much as intercourse was desirable, we agreed never to engage in it. I have a much better appreciation of the pressures teenagers must face when they become so close to another. She arrived at the decision to limit our physical expressions before I did. We discussed it, and I could accept the truth I was hearing and was happy to be living that truth in the days and years that followed. We are still best friends.

It stands to reason, of course, that one person's affection is another's foreplay, so there are no universally standardized lists of "acceptable affections." Furthermore, following Goergen's definitional schema, all affection is sexual. This, in turn, raises the question: How do vowed celibates define the term "sexual"? A brief response to the rhetorical question: There is no unanimous agreement.

Those who currently lecture on intimacy, sexuality, and celibacy, such as Maureen McCann, RSM, Fran Ferder, FSPA, and John Hegle, endorse Goergen's understanding of "sexual" as total personal presence to self and others, so many vowed celibates who have heard their presentations or have read Goergen's book define sexual in that broad context. Others equate sexual with genital behavior only. Still others vacillate between the two definitions. In my own clinical work with vowed celibates, I have learned never to assume what someone means when she or he refers to sexual behavior, but always to ask how that individual is using the term.

I was curious to see how vowed celibates define "sexual," so I included an item on my questionnaire that read: "Since making vows, I have engaged in behavior I would label 'sexual.'" I deliberately did not define the term, and several respondents approached me directly for clarification. "Answer it as you define it," I encouraged. For some, that was adequate; for others, it was not.

Some complained to me, "You seem to equate sexual with genital."

"Not necessarily," I responded. "You respond according to your own definition."

The majority completed the item without writing in a personal definition, so there is no way to know what they meant by the word. Those who *did* write in comments said, for the most part, that they had been sexual but had not engaged in intercourse. A typical comment is, "I have never had sexual intercourse. I have responded to your questions about 'physical involvement' with my image of my kind of involvement — kissing and touching" (44-year-old sister). A 52-year-old woman religious clarified her position by explaining, " 'Genital' is more clear a word for me or more specific than is sexual. I have not had intercourse but intimate affection that can lead to it." Finally, a sister, aged 54, wrote, "Sexual involvement — affective, warm, tender — nongenital. I think that is an important distinction — at least for me." Expressing his personal frustration with this section of the questionnaire, an order cleric wrote:

> The more I answered this part, the more its tone implied genitality. The definition of sexuality should have been given and its distinction from "genital involvement" should have been

made. I assume "sexual" need not mean genital. I don't think being "sexual" *has* to involve intercourse, orgasm, sexual arousal — especially intercourse and orgasm. (AGE 49)

Of course, in venting his frustration, this man defined the term.

Despite the consternation and ambiguity surrounding this item, 49 percent of the women and 62 percent of the men indicated having engaged in what they would call sexual behavior since making vows. Many spoke eloquently of their reactions to their experiences.

I found out that the physical aspect of sexuality wasn't as exciting and long-lasting as I had fantasized it to be. I found out that it really wasn't what I wanted. (SISTER, AGE 41)

At a time in my life when I switched ministries and became very isolated and overworked, I became sexually imbalanced and dabbled with pornography — magazines and video while travelling alone. It is a painful memory and I know I need a lot of healthy relationships and support to avoid making that kind of choice. In addition, I feel I am sexual with a woman now, but not in any genital way — through affectionate embraces and kisses. (DIOCESAN CLERIC, AGE 37)

The guilt I experienced wasn't worth the pleasure I received. I didn't feel free in this predicament though it took me awhile to work this through. (SISTER, AGE 61)

There's sex and there is loving. I thought before that I could transcend sex and just love. For a while by running away at the right times I escaped sex. Then I discovered I liked sex and fooled myself about the loving. Now (and I'm not finished growing and learning) I love, and I work to love. Sex can be a part of that to show affection and passion. It's only a part. It can be a very powerful urge but I've begun to find a place for it in something larger and more powerful. I make distinctions about sexual behavior — I choose not to have intercourse. It says something and could create a life that I'm not free to live. I'm sexually active within boundaries and with care. I am celibate. I am not married. I live a loving ministerial life. (ORDER PRIEST, AGE 39)

I learned from them [sexual experiences] not to be so curious or obsessed with the possibility or wonder what it's like. I'm over it, put the experiences in perspective, grown from them and out of them and am on with a deeper and more meaningful celibate life. (SISTER, AGE 40)

Some vowed celibates report their sexual experiences to be life-giving and sustaining, some claim that they are challenging, and others indicate that they are embarrassing and inappropriate to their vowed status. What seems a common thread through so many of the stories is a willingness to risk involvement within the context of relationship. Those who participated in my study who indicated sexual involvement tended, for the most part, to be sexually active for one or two years; several were or have been active for five years or more. The men reported more partners than did the women. An overwhelming number were sexual with other vowed celibates, and they claimed the interactions were mutually initiated or terminated. Very few reported a "one night stand," stereotypic fling. More of the women than the men had discontinued their sexual liaisons and most of the women and men both report ongoing friendships with their former sexual partners.

A gender difference, consistent with that held by women and men in general, emerged on an item asking about the most important aspect of the sexual interactions for respondents claiming such involvements. While an overwhelming majority of both women and men claimed the affectional component as most important, 20 percent of the men — as opposed to two percent of the women — named orgasm as most important. I suspect that there are two reasons for this: (1) the possibility that male celibates, like men in general, are more "act" conscious than are females, who tend to be more "contextual";[5] (2) the possibility that more of the male respondents defined sexual as genital and more of the female respondents defined sexual as total person.

That sexually active vowed celibates are discreet about their behaviors — however they define sexual — seems evident among my study participants. Over 90 percent of both women and men felt their activities were "secret." While I assume that this is probably true for most sexually involved celibates, I am aware of periodic scandals reported in the media that indicate that not all involved persons are as discreet or secret as they believe.

The media have also drawn attention to another aspect of vowed celibates' sexuality — sexual orientation. Some "guesstimates," similar to those proposed in Wolf's study, *Gay Priests*, speculate that 40 to 60 percent — or more — of Roman Catholic clergymen claim a homosexual orientation, and others predict an all-gay clergy by the turn of the century.[6] Current surveys do not support these figures. Sipe's 1990 research, *A Secret World: Sexuality and the Search for Celibacy*, reports 20 percent of male ministers to be homosexual men, and my own study revealed a 19 percent incidence of gay orientation among male ministers.[7] In addition, I found in my study that 9 percent of the men claimed an ambisexual and 72 percent claimed a heterosexual orientation. While Sipe and I may have polled groups that were not truly representative of male vowed celibates, I don't think it is coincidental that we came up with almost identical findings. Current investigations of sexual orientation among men in general place the incidence of male homosexuality at anywhere between 10 and 13 percent of the male population,[8] which is lower than that reported for male vowed celibates. However, the difference is not as striking or overwhelming as many would claim.

Eighty-seven percent of the women who responded to my study claimed a heterosexual orientation, 1 percent professed a lesbian orientation, and 12 percent claimed an ambisexual orientation. As Jeannine Gramick discusses in *Homosexuality in the Priesthood and Religious Life*, there are many reasons why more men than women claim a gay orientation.[9] Men tend to arrive at decisions about their orientations earlier in life than do women. Culture allows more fluid guidelines for women than men in terms of touch and affection. Also, more women than men eschew rigid categorizing regarding sexual orientation, claiming to love *persons* for themselves rather than gender assignment on the basis of orientation.[10] Finally, there is greater reluctance among women to come out as lesbians than among men to come out as homosexuals, a reluctance that may have been operative among the female respondents.

Some curious results emerged when respondents indicated the sex of their partners. Among the 49 percent of women religious acknowledging sexual behaviors, 39 percent report *only* male partners and 35 percent indicate *only* female partners, with the remaining 26 percent reporting partners of both sexes. What underlies the apparent contradiction between professed sexual orientation and actual behaviors reported?

Perhaps labels are truly not important to women. Maybe, as this 57-year-old sister who had three female partners and called herself heterosexual explains, the involvements were "situational":

> For the sexual involvements I have had with women, these were usually at times of great vulnerability and need. The episodes were short-lived. One of these women has remained my closest friend long after we terminated our sexual, physical involvement.

In some cases, vowed women learn about their affections, sexuality, and sexual orientation over a period of many years, which seems to have happened with this 49-year-old sister who claimed to be heterosexual while reporting sexual encounters exclusively with women (notice that her struggle is not yet resolved):

> These incidents happened when I was very young, although mature enough to choose otherwise. It was an emotional attraction — a "puppy love" attraction — that could very well have happened with a man, except that I was with all women many of those formative years. It was a time of great vulnerability and much confusion about feelings and the expression of those feelings. Still sexual fantasies occur, but no "action." I feel cheated in my past of having a better start on sexually related matters between sexes. As a naturally affectionate person, it seemed the ultimate in physical expression of that affection. I still get "mad" inside when I wonder why it cannot be expressed — even in a vowed life (yes, I know it's conflicting) — and even to another woman if that happens to be the case. I struggle with it yet. I have had recent doubts (because of my fantasies) if I am really gay. This stuff is really hard to say. It has been wonderful, though, in my best friend relationship. There is no sexual attraction — just wonderful, warm affection, total trust, and a real comfortableness. Affection is expressed warmly, but not genitally. It doesn't appear this will ever change. That is a wonderful feeling.

Data for the male respondents are a bit different. Of the 62 percent who reported being sexually active, 32 percent said their partners were exclusively male and 58 percent exclusively female. Again, actual behaviors do not necessarily coincide with reported orientation, and vice versa. In addition, all vowed celibates, whether gay, straight, or ambisexual, have to make decisions about the appropriateness of their behaviors. A brother claiming homosexual orientation told his story:

> I have to admit my own involvement was homosexual in nature and very scary. I was torn between feeling good and feeling guilty. Part of my own actions was to help my friend to feel better about himself (a wrong way to go). After my initial curiosity, the sex part was no longer important, but it still is to my friend. We struggle, but we aren't clear where we are moving except that I refuse the sexual activity. He doesn't want to hurt me. Celibacy is important and a countercultural witness to the world. For me as a religious, it provides me the opportunity to be a truly unique presence. It is a gift, but sometimes a very hard one to accept. (AGE 35)

Exploring the role of sexuality in their celibate lives, both women and men have to determine what these behaviors and attitudes mean in terms of their vocational commitments. As in so many issues discussed up to this point, there is no universal agreement on how they answer their question. Some say they can't live with the guilt and others say they could never have survived in ministry without having had the experiences. Some are embarrassed and some celebratory. In my study, the majority of women and men reported that their sexual involvements had a negligible impact on their vowed lives or that they served to strengthen their vocations. A few wrote in comments such as "I was very confused" or "This experience started my journey into what sexuality means to me" or "I began to see how I might be feminine, desirable... *and* celibate. It hasn't been easy." One sister, 40 years old, wrote, "It deepened my understanding of being human and deepened my understanding of the pain of the call to celibacy as it is defined by most people today."

What about Celibacy?

Those persevering in the discussion so far probably have some understandable questions: What about celibacy? Do these women and men take their vows seriously? Does all this mean that priests and women and men religious can be as sexually active as they want, as long as they don't give scandal or get married? Does it mean that committed celibates should avoid all relationships? There are no easy answers, and it appears that vowed celibates struggle with ambiguity surrounding their vow of celibacy just as they wrestle with the "fuzziness" of intimacy, appropriate affection, and sexuality. A 44-year-old sister noted, "I think that the pervasive ambiguity about sexuality in our culture has affected our understanding/judgments about celibacy."

Sandra Schneiders notes that celibacy at one time was the least "problematic" of the three vows because of the clear boundaries of denial and repression defining it:

It regulated affectivity by almost total denial, if not outright repression, and its obligations were perfectly clear. It was relatively simply to maintain this situation as long as religious life remained a closed system. But today celibacy has to be thought about in the context of the affective revolution that characterizes our time.[11]

As the closed system opens, new questions, challenges, and confusions emerge, and all of these are compounded even more for diocesan clergy, whose tradition, unlike that of vowed women and men in canonical institutes, has not consistently endorsed celibacy as instrinsic to the vocation and its lifestyle. Schneiders proposes what this means to all celibates today:

Although religious are playing a genuinely prophetic role in the affective transformation of society, many men and women celibates find it much more difficult to tackle their own personal affective transformation. Intimacy, with people of their own or the other sex, is unfamiliar territory for many religious. Much of the affective energy that was sublimated into compulsive work for so many years is hard to tap for the development of loving relationships with other individuals and within community. A long indoctrination in avoidance of deep relationships with those outside the community has made it unusually difficult for many religious to enter freely into close friendships with nonmembers. Lack of experience with their own affective responses causes upsetting reactions when religious who have allowed themselves virtually no affective expression since early adolescence find themselves suddenly in a two-sex world. Vocational disasters have been frequent enough in the last few years to give even the non-scrupulous some pause. Nevertheless, one senses a general commitment among women and men religious to their own sexual and affective maturation and to the creation of loving communities which bodes well for the future of religious life.[12]

As Schneiders discusses in chapter 7 of *New Wineskins*, numerous definitions of and reasons for celibacy have existed throughout history, including spouse of Christ, availability for ministry, and countercultural witness. Added to this, of course, is the oft-repeated lament of many diocesan clerics, "Because I have to as a requirement of being a priest today!"

I have found through my research and workshop contacts that all four definitions remain active among today's vowed celibates, but that the most commonly endorsed of all is "availability for ministry." Some report that they shift from definition to definition, depending upon where they are developmentally, both spiritually and psychologically. When asked directly, 90 percent of both male and female study respondents reported that they believe celibacy for diocesan clergy should be optional. An order priest, aged 63, wrote, "Celibacy has very little sign value to people in the Church. No harm would be done if it were abolished." "One question I ask myself," said a 41-year-old order priest, "is if celibacy is optional for diocesan clergy, would I choose to remain a religious or transfer to a diocesan priest with the option for marriage?" Finally, another order priest, aged 37, reported, "Celibacy is difficult, painful, but life-giving when I allow others to enter into my life. I would have difficulty being a priest and married, and I believe celibacy should be optional."

There are some vowed celibates who maintain that their interactions with others should be formal and professional so that personal intimacy does not become a threat. The majority, at least as far as my research and personal contact indicate, feel that they should pursue meaningful relationships — with risk of potential physical involvement — but they should make every effort to remain celibate.

Some vowed celibates — more men than women — maintain that it is possible to be sexually active and celibate simultaneously; others disagree. Much confusion surrounds the question, both personally and institutionally. For example, a 42-year-old order priest said, "I don't agree with the 'third way' [phenomenon of being a vowed celibate in a primary, genitally active, intimate relationship] even though it's been the pattern of my life." Some claim that celibacy is a growth process, others say it comes down to discipline:

> I have some struggling to remain celibate, but that's part of life, I think. I have a feeling that some think celibacy is an ideal and not possible. Somewhere here there would be a denial of the marvelous power of God in our lives (grace). And beyond other considerations, there is the whole question of faithfulness to one's commitment. (ORDER PRIEST, AGE 52)

To be appropriately intimate, affectionate, sexual, and celibate is a learning process for many vowed celibates who may eventually have to make serious vocational decisions about what is primary and workable in their lives that leaves them with a sense of authentic integrity. This learning process may take years, and the discernment is never easy. Pamela Bjorklund, a licensed clinical psychologist and spiritual director from San Jose who works with many vowed celibates, believes that it is not possible to have two primary relationships — commitments — at the same time over a long period. Eventually, says Bjorklund, neither commitment is really primary, or else one commitment actually becomes the context for living out the other, the primary, commitment.[13] A visual example of this would be the "two faces or a vase" picture, which most of us have seen in introductory psychology textbooks; either we see the two faces and the vase becomes background (context), or else we see the vase and the two faces become background (context). Both cannot remain prominent simultaneously. Speaking to this concept, a 64-year-old sister wrote:

I have seen only one person who has been sexually active and remained a committed celibate over a period of years. Usually, if it is ongoing and frequent, sexual activity prevails and committed celibacy gives way. Although in some instances after a long period of time juggling both, some give up sexual activity and re-commit themselves to celibacy. As religious superior and spiritual director I have seen this.

Arriving at acceptable conclusions about a personal stance toward celibacy and intimacy and sexuality is not easy, as the next two comments illustrate:

Currently I struggle between the shoulds and should nots and lots of black-and-white rules and regulations on one side and my natural instincts and desires on the other. Somewhere in between these two points on either end of the spectrum I know there's a point where the Lord and I need to agree on acceptable, appropriate behaviors for me that are guilt free. (SISTER, AGE 48)

I'm working on this stuff. I have an issue with saying one thing with my body (intimacy) which I don't feel I back up completely with my life. Also, discrepancy between celibate life-style and sexual activity with another. (DIOCESAN PRIEST, AGE 43)

Some vowed celibates see celibacy as a source of personal growth. For example, a woman religious, age 47, explained:

Although celibacy has often created a sense of existential loneliness within me, it has also brought forth from me an inner strength and empathy. I do not think I would have developed these qualities without the impetus of celibacy. Sometimes it would have often been much easier to act out physically/sexually than to face issues and be creatively supportive without intimate contact.

Another, a 35-year-old order priest, said:

Celibacy imposed by a structure, institution, or ministry is accepted by the "young" because of their desire for their vocational call/choice. But until celibacy is accepted as a personal value — for me — it remains imposed from the outside. Once I accept celibacy as a personal way of living life, I become free and celibacy becomes one of the ways I define myself as human — as disciple.

As frequently noted, there are no easy nor universally accepted answers to profound definitional questions. While the majority of vowed celibates do not approve of promiscuity, they do not agree on what celibacy is or how it should be lived. One sister, age 46, wrote, "I think it is wrong for anyone, vowed or not, to be jumping in and out of bed." I'm sure she would hear little disagreement for her opinion. On the other hand, this 54-year-old sister might spark a lively debate with her observation:

Celibacy as we have understood it — and as it is lived — and as it is *imposed* — is anachronistic. Whether it will survive — or *should* — I leave to the next movement of grace.

Summary

Where does all this leave us?

There are no absolutes emerging from the comments and observations of this chapter, but there are some clear trends of vowed celibates actively pursuing authentic answers to their existential reality of being intimate, affectionate, sexual, and celibate. They are searching for answers, falling in love, seeking appropriate expressions for their feelings, challenging their early training, and manifesting a willingness to live with the consequences of their behaviors. Some find their efforts toward growth to be painful and embarrassing; others find them life-giving. Many believe that intimacy and sexuality are essential to their effectiveness as authentic ministers. Others feel that sexuality and celibacy are incompatible. It seems that, for many, sexuality and celibacy are processes that are "grown into" as vowed women and men learn about themselves and their lives as they mature through adulthood. Further discussion of these issues will continue in subsequent chapters. For now, I will leave this chapter as I began it: There are no easy answers.

Chapter 4

PERSONALITY TYPES
AND THE ROAD
TO RELATIONSHIPS

Despite years of formation training that militated against intimate relationships and prescribed only professional interpersonal interactions, middle-aged vowed celibates today seek to develop and actively cherish meaningful intimate relationships that are warm and affectionate — and that are more similar to women's ways of relating than they are to men's. For some, this observation is cause for celebration, "Gee, isn't it great that they feel free to pursue what they really value!" For others, it is cause for consternation, "I knew it! Priests and brothers aren't 'real men,' and nuns will never make it as 'soldiers of Christ!'"

Does the fact that celibate males value intimacy indicate that they are less masculine than men in general? I know plenty of ministers who would object vehemently to the mere suggestion. Likewise, does the reality that celibate females function productively in careers imply that they are less feminine than women in general? Again, loud protests would erupt. As long ago as 1978, Alvarez found that Catholic sisters were more androgynous than women in general, which undoubtedly explained and facilitated their professional success.[1] Might not the male celibates, if given the same instrument Alvarez used with women, manifest an appreciation for "women's ways of being" that facilitates their efforts toward meaningful intimacy? In fact, this seems to be the case.

To understand the implications of this and to develop a vocabulary for the concepts involved, we will have to take a somewhat technical stroll through the history of gender stereotyping and psychological testing.

Masculinity/Femininity — The History

Just as the sexual revolution that began in the 1960s challenged centuries of sexual attitudes, the gender revolution that emerged at the same time also questioned long-held beliefs concerning masculine men and feminine women.[2] While the debate is far from over, scholars from various disciplines have been able to study stereotypical masculinity and femininity to identify the nonconscious limitations inherent in each.

A classic study by Broverman in the early 1970s found that mental health professionals equated healthy male (masculine) adjustment with healthy adult development, but not with healthy female (feminine) development.[3] Women were trapped in a double bind: If they were emotionally adjusted females, they were not emotionally adjusted adults; if they were emotionally adjusted adults, they were not emotionally adjusted females. Later replications of the Broverman study, despite intervening years of "human liberation," yielded no significant changes in attitudes and mixed findings regarding actual therapist behaviors toward male and female clients.[4]

While masculine men subscribing to the male-as-normative mystique reap numerous social and cultural benefits, they also pay a great price. Premature strokes and heart attacks, long accepted as "unfortunate but necessary" results of hard work and dedication, are now being targeted as possible evidence of overwork and overachievement. High suicide rates for men, escalating divorce rates, increased attention to males' lack of best friends, and other interpersonal problems suggest that stereotypic masculinity has limitations, just as stereotypic femininity does.

If these images of femininity and masculinity are so hurtful and limiting to both women and men, then where did they come from and what has sustained them for so long? To answer this in depth from all academic disciplines is beyond the scope of this discussion, but a brief overview of some recent summaries can help construct a broad backdrop that enhances understanding. Since more has been written about men than women (part of the legacy of nonconscious sexism for more than three thousand years is the belief that women were not "total" human persons and were, therefore, not worthy of or worth study), we will begin the conversation with a description of what makes men masculine.

To be credibly masculine in what Schaef calls the male system, a man must exhibit strength, independence, confidence, success, logic, and assertiveness. He is expected to control himself and others, to remain emotionally detached and financially sound. He abhors weakness in any form — physical, intellectual, emotional, social, or spiritual — and is supposed to be an expert on just about everything. Schaef's male system man has changed in content but not in form throughout recorded history.

As Doyle points out in chapter 2 of *The Male Experience*,[5] core characteristics of masculinity in the Western world have shifted during the centuries. In the Golden Age of Greek and early Roman civilization, "real men" were Adonis-like gods, athletic, well-muscled, well-educated warriors who valued male companionship and competition. Masculinity as physical prowess in Greek times yielded to masculinity as spiritual growth during the Middle Ages, an epoch that embraced Christian values exemplified by stringent spiritual disciplines in search of holiness. The gaunt mortifier who pursued an ascetic life of prayer replaced the muscle-bound warrior as the "real man" of the times. Both athletes and ascetes were then displaced by the entrepreneurs of the eighteenth century, the "real men" who turned profits, increased holdings, and accumulated wealth. Affluence became the hallmark of masculinity, and the richer men became, the more leisurely they lived. "Real men" of that era were wealthy, socially powerful, and pampered; ostensibly genteel and mannerly at home, they were ruthless in the marketplace.

Masculinity in U.S. and Canadian culture is a curious combination of the well-heeled entrepreneur, spiritually motivated religious exile, optimistic immigrant, and the rough-and-tumble pioneer cowboy. Men in this male system believe they can fashion their destinies through hard work, clever business deals, and periodic "stretching" of the rules. So today's real man is supposed to be an athlete, a cowboy, and CEO of a Fortune 500 company *and*, because of the recent gender revolution, is also expected to become a warm and nurturing husband and father when he crosses the threshold of his home at night.

Throughout all these historical epochs, women were alternately perceived as chattel, seductresses, emotional supports, or biological necessities. If they stepped out of their appointed roles, they were disciplined by men who truly believed it was their task to control and take care of women.

How does an infant boy become a strong and independent man who knows how to "look out for number one," make decisions, and beat out the competition? In short, how does he learn about and succeed in the male system today?

Combining several theories to answer the question, we can say that the boy's journey into acceptable male system status begins before he is born when he is identified by over 80 percent of first-time parents as the preferred sex.[6] Once on the scene, he experiences an amazing array of nonconscious behaviors that launch him on his way. Described as sturdy and strong, he is handled and played with more roughly than a girl baby and given boys' action toys. He is generally cared for more by his mother (since his father, a real man in the male system, has learned that babies are women's work) and, subsequently, sees himself as one with her. He, like all infants, merges with his primary caretaker and enjoys a symbiotic relationship with her, viewing her as an extension of himself and identifying as one with her while wallowing in a wonderful relationship of love, care, support, and nurturance.

Mother, for her part, knows from the lessons of the system that she is responsible for raising a credible masculine man, so she cannot allow her son to remain too close to her for too long without risk of creating a "momma's boy," a son "tied to her apron strings," a "sissy," or a "wimp." To avoid this, mother must teach her son that he can *not* continue to identify as one with her because to do so would be to learn how to be like her — female and feminine — rather than what he must become — masculine. "For his own good," she begins to push him away from her, physically and emotionally, thus breaking the bond of closeness he has enjoyed since birth.

For the male child, then, his first experience of relationship is one of abandonment — abandonment at the hands of a woman — a wrenching at the preverbal level that, according to some theorists, lays the foundation for a lifetime of mistrust of both women and relationships. (*If* fathers would do more parenting, of course, they could teach their sons men's ways without imposing the loss of relational ties, warmth, and trust.) Cultural forces coalesce to instruct the boy about his life's task, teaching him that he must take care of himself ("Get out there and hit him back!"), that he must be productive ("What are you going to be when you grow up?"), invulnerable ("Quit your crying — it doesn't hurt that bad!"), privileged ("Of course he can! He's a boy, isn't he?"), and competent ("Stand up straight. Do you want people to think you're a sissy?"). Action toys and busy bedroom decor proclaim to him that he can — and must — *do*, must *act* on his environment, figure how it works, and know how to fix it when it breaks. Playing boyhood games in groups teaches him cooperation for the sake of competition, and quibbling about the rules ("Was the ball in, on, or outside the line?") serves as a type of boot camp for adulthood marketplace negotiation. Progressing through his gender stereotyping lessons, he learns that achievement and self-assuredness are important, and that he conveys these by presenting himself as confident and successful. He also learns that feelings, except for anger, make him vulnerable, and that girls are the enemy.

By late childhood, around the ages of 9 to 12, he enters into the developmental stage of the "best friend," that special time in growing up when he is cognitively and emotionally mature enough to reflect on and share himself with another in a peer relationship characterized by the exchange of secrets. Trusting that his friend will respect confidentiality, the boy risks self-disclosure — the real "stuff" of intimacy — only to discover that it's *not* safe. His best friend, the kid with whom he'd laughed and played, the one who promised to keep his mouth shut, commits the ultimate betrayal by violating confidentiality — usually for purposes of self-advancement. The best friend, in other words, uses the secrets as social bartering chips in the competitive male system game of one-up-manship. Our developing male has now suffered his second major relational disappointment; the first was in infancy when he was denied continued access to identification with his mother, and the second is his rude awakening in late childhood that others — even males — can't be trusted. He has learned that it is better to have buddies and pals with whom he shares events and things than it is to have friends before whom he is vulnerable.

The groundwork for male system education now completed,

the young male finishes adolescence and moves into young adult-hood according to plan. To take care of himself as he looks out for number one, he selects a career, proves that he can stand inde-pendently, trusts almost no one, denies feelings, and disguises fear and insecurity. He maintains personal and interpersonal control by quantifying and compartmentalizing his life, even his relation-ships. He learns to equate intimacy with sex and self-disclosure with weakness and to measure his self-worth by the size of his paycheck and the status of his position in the social, economic, or ecclesiastical hierarchy. Succeeding in the male system, now a real man with masculine traits believed to be genetically transmitted and willed by God, he personifies what the system has told him: His experience is the human experience, what a person is to be like, and that it is his right and duty to force others into his way of being or else to treat them as deviant or deficient. He fashions economic, political, legal, social, and ecclesiastical structures to re-flect and justify his perceptions. Of course, he pays a tremendous cost for his beliefs and behaviors since he is not permitted to emote or relate or nurture; but, since his system does not value these, he concludes that they are not very important.

Inherent in male system perspectives are dualisms and hierar-chies, so if males must be masculine, which is normative (recall the Broverman study), then females must be feminine, a state embody-ing all the opposite traits, which, hierarchically, are deemed less valuable but complementary.[7] Thus, the nonrelational, logical, un-emotional masculine male requires a relational, illogical, emotional feminine female. As the antithesis of masculine, feminine is cast as compliant, passive, nurturing, weak, dependent, and emotional, and the female's upbringing and training are nonconsciously de-signed to prepare her to assume these characteristics.

Like her brother, she begins life totally immersed in relation-ship with mother and enjoys all the warmth, touch, and nurturance involved. But unlike her brother, she does not have to sever her ties with her caretaker to learn her role; she learns by remaining in that primary bond. Keenly attuned to the "stuff" of relating as she expe-riences and observes her mother's sensitivity toward and support of others, she develops a broad repertoire of emotional responses and a finely honed sense of the other. Her games and bedroom decor communicate that she should "be" rather than "do" since they emphasize attractiveness and even fussiness. Any action toys that might be given her are generally action in the service of others, such as miniature baking sets, imitation housecleaning toys, and sewing kits. Through observing mother and other women around her, the female child comes to appreciate the interconnectedness of life as she hears about the impact of one person's behavior (maybe dad's temper) on others (perhaps mom's moodiness, brother's school, or uncle's drinking).

While her brother is playing group games learning cooperation for the sake of competition, she is more often playing one-on-one with another girl and is learning that the quality of relationship is far more important than winning a game. In fact, she will probably stop a game if she fears its continuation will jeopardize the friendship.

Growing through childhood, she sees that her status and worth are dependent upon the status and worth of the people with whom she associates. When she reaches the late childhood stage of the best friend, she discovers that her confidences are betrayed for the sake of her best friend's securing a higher status relationship. Later, in adolescence and young adulthood, her value as person — so she is told — depends on the worth of the men she dates or the man she eventually marries.

Throughout her developmental years, the girl receives a Catch-22 message: She is valued for being feminine — relational, emotional, nurturing — but she is less valuable because she is feminine and not masculine. *But*, if she is masculine, then she violates her nature as feminine!

What all this reduces to is the reality that the male system has a strongly vested interest in maintaining its supply of feminine women to support its cadre of masculine men. Stereotypic femininity and masculinity are sexist because they oppress women and men both, denying them access to the full range of human expression. However, because male system philosophy is predicated upon the assumption that it is rooted in a natural order designed by God, it defies scrutiny by threatening its critics with accusation of blasphemy and is entrenched in both Church and culture.

Psychologists studying personality between the 1940s and 1960s participated in nonconscious sexism by assuming and proclaiming the inviolability and correctness of masculine men and feminine women. Buying into prevailing cultural beliefs, they subscribed to the notion that feminine men and masculine women were "abnormal" — in fact, that they were homosexual or lesbian, an orientation considered pathological until December 1973, when the American Psychiatric Association dropped homosexuality from its list of diagnostic categories.

Psychologists of that era tried to develop psychological tests to measure masculinity and femininity in the hopes (sometimes overtly and sometimes covertly articulated) of devising a tool that could reliably diagnose homosexuality.[8] Their selection of items for masculinity-femininity scales reflected four assumptions: (1) that masculinity and femininity were biologically determined rather than learned; (2) that masculinity and femininity were opposite ends of a single "gender continuum" rather than multidimensional behavioral variables; (3) that movement in a direction other than "gender appropriate" behavior was indicative of homosexuality; (4) that the very concepts of masculinity for men and femininity for women were in the natural order of life and, therefore, the only correct ways for humans to behave.

Items for M-F scales were riddled with cultural stereotypes that seem almost ludicrous today. For example, respondents elevated their masculinity scores if they endorsed liking outdoor sports, reading hot rod magazines, and tinkering with cars; likewise, they elevated their femininity scores if they endorsed being bothered by the sight of blood or rodents, enjoying playing with children, or crying easily at sad movies.

Despite repeated efforts to measure masculinity and femininity and to correlate these qualities with mental health and/or sexual orientation, psychologists failed. They discovered many masculine women and feminine men who were emotionally healthy heterosexuals as well as masculine men and feminine women who were emotionally healthy homosexuals or lesbians. As time passed and study data accumulated, psychologists learned that respondents' masculinity or femininity scores more often reflected occupational interests than sexual orientation.[9]

Other behavioral science research, notably that of Margaret Mead, challenged the assumptions behind traditional measures of masculinity and femininity, especially the belief that biology is the determinant of gender-appropriate behavior.[10] Mead's most striking findings came from her studies of the Arapesh, Mudagumor, and Tchambuli of New Guinea, three groups whose behavior patterns were blatantly inconsistent with prevailing Western expectations of gender-appropriate behavior: Arapesh men and women were both "feminine," Mudagumor men and women were both "masculine," and Tchambuli men were "feminine" while the women were "masculine." Mead's findings directly refute the "anatomy as destiny" model of gender-appropriate behavior, which was (and for many still is) implicit in Western psychologists' understanding of human behavior.

In short, there are many problems with traditional conceptions and measurements of masculinity and femininity that continue to plague professionals and lay people alike.

Androgyny Today

Sandra Bem attempted to address some of these difficulties by developing a measure of psychological androgyny, the *Bem Sex Role Inventory*, a self-report paper-and-pencil checklist of behaviors.[11] Bem predicated her construction of the instrument on a two-dimensional rather than the traditional one-dimensional understanding of masculinity and femininity. In other words, the one-dimensional approach sees masculinity and femininity as opposite ends of a single continuum on which individuals are "more or less" one or the other, and that either extreme, by definition, is mutually exclusive of the other. It could be graphically depicted as follows:

masculinity ⟵——————————————⟶ *femininity*

The two-dimensional approach, on the other hand, sees each as independent of the other; in this approach individuals can come out one of four ways: high masculine/high feminine (androgynous), high masculine/low feminine (masculine), high feminine/low masculine (feminine), or low masculine/low feminine (undifferentiated). The two-dimensional model is graphically depicted as follows:

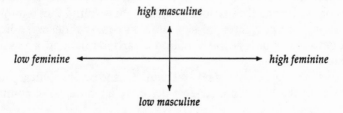

high masculine

low feminine ⟵——————————————⟶ *high feminine*

low masculine

Respondents rate themselves on a number of characteristics considered socially desirable for women (e.g., cheerful, warm) and men (e.g., self-reliant, competitive) on a Likert-type scale from 1 (never or almost never) to 7 (always or almost always). Their results are calculated, then compared to the median scores of Bem's standardization sample of Stanford women and men to yield a "designation" of masculine, feminine, undifferentiated, or androgynous.[12]

The *Bem* is not without its problems. First, as a self-report inventory, the *Bem* is subject to the vagaries of personal perception; some people rate themselves too high or too low or too inaccurately. Second, *Bem* items, even while two-dimensional, are nevertheless based on cultural stereotypes of socially acceptable gender behaviors, a construct that, according to those who want to get away from the value- and affect-laden concepts of masculinity and femininity, is inherently limiting.[13] Third, the standardization sample is composed of college students, a group that may not accurately reflect adult women and men in general.

Given these limitations, however, the *Bem* is valuable as a research tool to help people better understand their behaviors and attitudes. Numerous studies using *Bem* results in correlation with a variety of behaviors suggest that psychologically androgynous persons do, in fact, demonstrate a greater repertoire of responses in more situations than do those who are exclusively masculine or feminine or who are undifferentiated.[14] Androgyny in women is correlated with positive self-esteem and the ability to withstand pressure to conform; androgyny in men is correlated with good listening skills, nurturance, and empathy. It seems that psychologically androgynous people feel freer than do exclusively masculine or feminine people to employ responses appropriate to the situation rather than to their gender. Furthermore, Bem found that masculine women were also expressive (a traditional feminine behavior of "expressing emotions"), but that feminine men were *not* also agentic (a traditional masculine behavior of "getting things done"). Finally, Bem found that feminine women were not as expressive as either masculine or androgynous women unless the situation clearly demanded a passive nurturing stance.[15]

Even though there are several heuristic and philosophical problems with the *Bem*, data suggest there are advantages of comfort in freedom of expression among women and men who are not confined to culturally prescribed gender-appropriate behavior.

Study Results

As mentioned, social psychologist Jean Alvarez found that women religious were more androgynous than women in general and that their androgyny appeared to correlate positively with their ability to hold and successfully execute managerial/administrative positions — career tasks more generally associated with men. She raised the question, still unanswered today, whether androgynous women are attracted to religious life because other androgynous women are found there, or whether women religious become androgynous because of community and ministerial experiences.

A significant part of my study was the *Bem*, which I asked respondents to complete along with the eleven-page questionnaire.[16] I had three reasons for including the *Bem*: (1) to replicate Alvarez's study with today's middle-aged women religious; (2) to use the *Bem* with men religious and diocesan priests which, as far as I know, had never been done; (3) to investigate the extent to which measured sex role on the *Bem* would correlate with attitudes and behaviors regarding intimacy, sexuality, and celibacy.

	Femininity Score (5.5 cut-off)	Masculinity Score (4.8 cut-off)
Women (n = 236)	5.6314	4.9551*
Men (n = 97)	5.5392*	4.7660

TABLE 3.1. Group means for vowed celibates on *Bem*

*significant at p < .01 level.

Table 3.1 presents the results of averaging the group scores for respondents. When treated this way, the data indicate that as a group, the women religious who participated in this study came out androgynous and their masculinity score was significantly higher than the median cut-off score for women. As a group, the diocesan clerics and men religious came out feminine, and their femininity score was significantly higher than the median cut-off for men.[17] Comparing female and male celibates on their group scores, it is interesting to note that their femininity scores are not significantly different but that the women religious scored significantly higher than the men on the masculinity scale.[18]

Implications for Relationships

These results support Alvarez's earlier findings that women religious, as a group, are androgynous. They also indicate that priests and men religious, as a group, are feminine.[19] How might these results influence the discussion of relationships, sexuality, and celibacy for vowed celibates?

It seems, based on data generated by the questionnaire, that many middle-aged vowed celibates have developed an appreciation for relationship and prioritize quality time on a frequent basis to be with their best friends who are, for the most part, other vowed celibates. Most of these relationships are of long-standing duration. Although research respondents may not be representative of all vowed celibates, and while the number of male respondents is quite small, their responses suggest some interesting trends that are rippling the waters of relational growth in their lives today.

First, these celibates experienced formation programs that specifically forbade and punished close friendships (a male system attitude), yet they currently affirm intimacy as an important part of their adult lives (a female system attitude). This suggests that women religious have, for the most part, embraced their feminine valuation of relationship in spite of the masculine, hierarchical structuring of traditional religious life; it also suggests that the men religious and diocesan clerics have, for the most part, also transcended their male system experiences in both culture and Church to explore the value of relationships in their lives. It is likely that the men in this study, because they are more feminine than men in general, have learned to both appreciate and respect the female system characteristics that nurture and support intimacy. "Thank God we're getting away from the 'macho man boys' club' of my early training in the seminary!" said a diocesan priest, aged 49. "My relationship with my best friend, while difficult at times, has made me so much warmer, more appreciative of both women and men."

Second, the women and men who participated in my study report a female system definition of intimacy that equates intimacy with self-disclosure and mutuality. They indicate, unlike the men in McGill's study, being self-disclosing 50 percent or more of the time with their partners, and that their partners are equally self-disclosing in return. The women's androgyny and the men's femininity undoubtedly moved them beyond their early male system training of how to behave in relationships. Commenting on his own growth process in this respect, a 52-year-old order priest said:

> I was always fearful of getting involved with someone, male or female, because I was afraid of the potential for sexual involvement as well as the risk of saying "too much" that would come back to haunt me. I'd been hurt that way when I first entered the community, and another guy used something I'd told him to get himself out of a mess. For years after that, I was very careful — guarded. Now, through my friendship with another man in my community, I've learned to trust again, and feel like a new person because of it.

From a different perspective, a sister, aged 55, wrote:

> As a kid growing up, I learned that I was supposed to go along with what the other wanted — that was the way to have a friendship. Of course, I got stuck in lots of unhealthy relationships over the years, where I was too dependent and needy. I'm working on this. It has to be a shared effort or it's not really a friendship at all.

Third, it is likely that the men's femininity contributed to their freedom in selecting and naming other men as best friends, a rare phenomenon among men in general as reported in behavioral science literature. Does this happen because of their lived experience in community? Do shared values, rooted in a faith stance that generates a ministry of service and nurturance, free them to claim nonstereotypic friendships with other men? The question posed by Alvarez for women religious could also be asked of the men: Do psychologically feminine men go into ministry because they see others like them there, or do they become feminine because of their experiences in community and ministry? Perhaps future investigations involving larger male groups can address these questions.

Fourth, an overwhelming majority of both men and women in this study report engaging in behavior they would call "affectional," something expressly forbidden during their early training and a manifestation of "connectedness" not strongly endorsed by male system standards. Again, it seems plausible that the nontraditional stances of the women and men, as reflected in the *Bem* results, have contributed to their freedom of affectional expressions.

Fifth, for the women and men reporting sexual involvement, however vaguely that may be defined, it seems that their behaviors were or are part of long-standing relationships, consented to mutually, and, where terminated, terminated mutually. Such willingness to live with the struggle is inconsistent with male system standards wherein people are taught to divorce sex from sexuality, to insist that a dominant partner initiate and terminate the behaviors, and to perceive multiple episodes of casual sex for males to be normative. Speaking his own story to this very issue, a brother wrote:

> By my late twenties and early thirties, I was going crazy with sexual preoccupation. It's a long story, but I eventually left the congregation, and for the ten years I was out, I tried everything. You name it, I did it. But that just wasn't me, and I learned that lots of sex was not the answer for my problems and loneliness. I gave it a lot of thought, got some counseling, and re-entered the community. I now live a nongenital, celibate life. I'm not proud of those ten years, but can see it was something I had to do to get to where I am today. (AGE 50)

Finally, an overwhelming majority of respondents endorsed a process definition of celibacy wherein close relationships are valued and pursued, even at the risk of physical involvement, as essential to their authentic development as individuals. This is in contrast to both male system and early formation training exhorting professional distancing.

Whatever interpretations best fit the findings, it appears that vowed celibates, both women and men, view intimacy, sexuality, and celibacy very differently from men in general and the traditional training manuals for priests and religious taught in formation programs during the time these respondents underwent their training. The actual degree to which the women's androgyny or the men's femininity affect this is unknown. However, it seems safe to speculate that the women's and men's *Bem* results, which are different from the population at large, have some bearing on this finding. Neither the women nor the men appear to be locked into gender-appropriate "relationship games" despite their struggles with these as they matured into middle age. Respondents seem to be claiming themselves as *persons in relationship* who value intimacy and what it means to them as vowed celibates.

Some may be alarmed that the male respondents, as a group, came out feminine on the *Bem*. "Does this mean," they might ask, "that we're moving toward an effeminate clergy/brotherhood? Does this indicate the emergence of a gay clergy/brotherhood?" It is important to remember that the *Bem* measures *personality* expression, *not* sexual orientation. Furthermore, *feminine* behaviors are *not* the same as effeminate mannerisms. What the men's *Bem* results *do* suggest is that they are not traditional male system personality types who mistrust intimacy as self-disclosure and who establish strict boundaries around their interactions; rather, as a group, these men are appreciative of meaningful relationships, invest in them, and value them — whether they claim a gay, straight, or ambisexual orientation.

Likewise, that the women as a group came out androgynous on the *Bem* says nothing about their sexual orientation or their personal mannerisms. It *does* suggest that they, more than women in general, play an active role in initiating, nurturing, and terminating their relationships.

Finally, it is important to remember that there is a rich body of research correlating masculinity and femininity with occupational interests, and that men who enter professions in the arts, literature, and social service generally score higher in femininity than do men who pursue the sciences and business. Likewise, women who work as administrators score higher in masculinity than do those who are employed in nursing and education. In light of this, current *Bem* results are quite consistent with the types of work vowed celibates are doing today.

Concluding Comments

Some may find this chapter pretty dull reading and others may view it as an exciting breakthrough in the attempt to understand why celibate women and men value intimacy and struggle with sexuality and celibacy in a more female than male way. And, as always, the results would be most conclusive only if every vowed celibate in the United States and Canada completed both the *Bem* and the questionnaire.

I'd like to offer some observations on these results based on my contacts with vowed celibates in educational, renewal, and clinical settings. Again, these people are not necessarily representative of all ministers, yet conceivably they reflect the experiences of many.

Women religious are, for the most part, successful in their careers, even if they were not or are not always fond of the work. As a group, they are very well educated; most hold a bachelor's degree, many have a master's or a doctorate. Atypical of most other women their age, they have been active in careers since late adolescence or young adulthood, have pursued ongoing education, and have assumed leadership and managerial roles as they have advanced through the ranks. Their work generally demands male system skills and attitudes as they interact with civil and ecclesiastical leaders, generally males, in executing their duties. In addition, they grew up in congregations whose organization and discipline were predicated upon male system structures and values. That they would develop and express stereotypic masculine characteristics is not surprising and would certainly contribute to the elevation of their masculinity scores on the *Bem*.

While progressing through their careers, today's middle-aged women religious lived through the gender revolution of the 1970s and 1980s and raised their consciousness regarding rigidly restrictive sex stereotyping; they also received support to name, claim, and celebrate their attributes as women, especially their relational skills and sensitivities. As a result, they experienced conditions that allowed exploration and experimentation with both masculine and feminine expressions of themselves.

This does not imply that women religious move effortlessly into meaningful intimacy with personally acceptable sexual expression consistent with their understanding of celibacy. Products of their past, they sometimes found (and find) themselves in stereotypic relationships, with both women and men, assuming traditional, feminine, "passive" roles of dependency, one-way nurturance, and varying degrees of flirtatiousness. They may feel (and even appear to be) very adolescent in their initial attempts. On the other hand, their career-oriented, male system training may leave them more stereotypically masculine, striving to compartmentalize and control themselves and the other in relationship. Just as their growth as persons is developmental and unique, so too is their growth in relationships. There is no single nor sequential pattern for all.

Where women religious do seem to have advantages in the relational arena is in their freedom to experiment within supportive circles of similarly struggling women religious of comparable backgrounds who are exposed to ongoing education through reading, workshops, and retreat or renewal experiences. Many, active in some facet of the feminist movement, interact with a wide spectrum of lay women who also seek meaningful interpersonal interactions while engaging in productive careers, and so receive encouragement from another front for their efforts toward authentic intimacy. Less entrenched in traditional feminine tasks such as homemaking and child care, women religious seem to be freer than many women to meet a wide variety of people of both sexes and to apply a wider range of human (androgynous) interaction skills to their relational endeavors.

In summary, psychologically androgynous women religious have the potential to experience the best of both worlds: relational fulfillment predicated upon female system mutuality and career satisfaction rooted in male system competitive competency.

My contacts with vowed celibate males suggest a different set of experiences for them than for vowed celibate females. Many of the men feel, in their own words, trapped between their own and others' expectations. Their choice for ministry, a service-oriented, nurturing, and supportive vocation, is atypical for men raised in male system ethics of competition and achievement, and to be effective ministers they must exhibit characteristics more commonly associated with traditional femininity. They value and pursue relationships that encompass more than the buddy or pal associations of traditional masculine interactions, and many say that they are not interested in power, parish finances, or leadership positions. Several manifest finely tuned sensitivities more frequently associated with females than with males.

Because of these values, psychologically feminine men are a threat to the male system, which inherently strives to protect and perpetuate itself. Men and women both, conditioned from early childhood to believe that the male system is the correct and superior system, nonconsciously marshall their resources to bring these feminine (read: deviant) men back into line with mainstream masculinity, and do so through ridicule and intimidation. Thus, allegations of homosexuality and weakness are hurled at feminine male ministers to humiliate them into socially "acceptable" male behavior or to dismiss them as unworthy of serious attention. Although they may be excellent ministers and friends, they are rejected as human adults worth taking seriously.

In other words, psychologically feminine vowed celibate men have a more difficult time being accepted by society than do psychologically androgynous vowed celibate women. The nonconscious sexism operating here is the tacit assumption that it is okay for women to be like men, as long as they are also feminine, but that it is *not* okay for men to be like women, especially when they are not also masculine. To phrase it another way, it seems that today's middle-aged women religious have the potential for the double bonus of satisfying, mutual relationships *and* successful careers, whereas today's middle-aged priests and brothers suffer the tension of deciding between either rewarding relationships *or* successful careers. Of course, there is no way of knowing just how many celibate men are psychologically feminine, nor is there any way of knowing — based on current data — how these men fare over time. Additional research with larger groups would help to answer these questions.

It is important to remember that numbers and percentages sometimes obfuscate the real issues — that, in this case, people are working hard to make sense out of some very confusing experiences and insights. What they were told to expect, and how they were instructed to behave, simply did not work for them as they moved into relationships they identified as life-giving and essential. Growth in intimacy, like growth in any area of human development, takes time, commitment, and a willingness to risk mistakes. Many vowed celibates are making that investment.

Chapter 5

PREDICTABILITY WITHIN THE CHAOS

I presently struggle with the lived experience that within the celibate commitment I find a partner/friend/lover or companion desirable and helpful, but not sure it can be done within a practical context. [It is] presently raising questions: (1) must I leave one commitment in order to have a partner or (2) is there a way for my commitment to continue and yet have the ability to be intimate at all levels, including sexually/genitally, with one other person in a love relationship? I find a partner/friend/lover or companion can make me an even more effective, loving, compassionate minister. (BROTHER, AGE 45)

There needs to be more openness among women religious concerning sexual drives as well as a more intensive support system. (SISTER, AGE 50)

I think it's important to follow through if you promise not to do something. It's not that you can't make mistakes, if you realize they *are* mistakes. Sex isn't dirty or evil, but you have to find the level of expression appropriate to the relationship and state of life, a common Christian task. (ORDER PRIEST, AGE 40)

I still believe that celibacy — single-heartedness — is the best route for priesthood and religious life. My own personal failures do not lessen my conviction about this value. (DIOCESAN PRIEST, AGE 53)

I learned about the "beauties" and "bads" of friendship the hard way, but it was worth it. It felt good to be human. Today I see celibacy as gift for me. Through all the joy, pain, and confusion, I feel whole and fulfilled but still in the process of *trying* to live celibate life on a daily basis. (SISTER, AGE 52)

Relationships — wonderful and wearisome, delightful and painful, life-giving and death-dealing — are vital to vowed celibates today.[1] How they approach and experience them is highly unique, yet they demonstrate enough similarities that a few general overview observations are possible.

Middle-aged vowed celibates straddle two profoundly different cultural milieux: (1) the pre–Vatican II world of sexual repression and institutionalized gender-appropriate behaviors and (2) the post–Vatican II world of sexual liberation, ambiguous gender-appropriate behaviors, the human potential movement, and process theology. They try to balance their personal journeys in adult development with their corporate journey as vowed celibates in a Church-in-transition; on both fronts, they are explorers entering a new land without benefit of maps or guides. They know what they were taught as youngsters, but question the applicability of their early training to their daily adult wanderings; they know where they've been, but are not always sure of where they are going. A common theme is articulated by many in their quest for wholeness: that insights, decisions, and confusions have emerged over time, and new information demands new commitments and questions.

If the people who attend workshops and who participated in my study are at all representative of vowed celibates in general, then the fact that the overwhelming majority claimed having a best friend is amazing in light of their cultural and religious heritage, and is even more amazing for the men than the women. In other words, the men received a double-dose proscription against intimacy — from male system culture and Church — yet somehow managed to embrace intimacy in their adult lives and to treat it as necessary and important. Meaningful intimacy for both women and men is undoubtedly related to their personality type, as a group, according to the *Bem*, and to their adult developmental struggles.

As androgynous women and feminine men, study participants are claiming to be free of culturally prescribed stereotypic restrictions of gender-appropriate behaviors. These women are less likely to be passive and dependent; the men, less likely to be distant and autonomous. For both, there is freedom and challenge to enter into the profound risk of vulnerability before another. How did this happen, and what might it mean?

The Developmental Picture

According to developmental psychologists, the cornerstone of any individual's ability to relate to another is trust.[2] Children learn trust by interacting with parents, siblings, relatives, and neighbors, all of whom teach them that the world is predictable and safe by caring for them in responsible and supportive ways. They establish and honor limits with children and love children unconditionally as they respond to the youngsters' physical, emotional, and psychological needs. Not everyone extends these idyllic conditions to all children at all times, but if enough do, then children feel safe with others.

Beyond this general observation, psychologists have shockingly little to say about how humans are attracted to one another, how they initiate their movements toward another, or how they maintain relationships over the long haul. There are many descriptive works outlining basic patterns of attraction and relationship development and deterioration, but almost none that are explanatory, giving the reasons behind the success or failure of interpersonal interactions.

For example, social psychologists have found that people are attracted to each other if they have similar interests and complementary needs.[3] However, as Knapp points out, needs change constantly.[4] Thus, the attractiveness of others is constantly shifting, and relationships based upon task need (attraction to another because she or he can help with a given job) may not sustain social need (attraction to another because *you* are in the mood for a party and so is the other).

It is not surprising that relationship studies are so disappointing. This is because the majority of them treat relationship as product rather than process, a perspective perpetuated by the culturally promulgated myth that relationships just happen if the chemistry is right. This short-sighted view oversimplifies the reality of a very complex and mysterious phenomenon.

In general, the cultural timetable for relationship development assumes that children learn trust very early in life, gradually move into social interactions with others during elementary school, and then, during late childhood, begin to have a best friend, most often a person of the same sex. After that, so the cultural myth goes, girls and boys begin to notice one another, fall in and out of puppy love with varying degrees of sexual experimentation during their teen years, then magically meet the right person to whom, because of some inexplicable attraction, they entrust their futures with the expectation that they will live together in storybook bliss for the rest of their lives. Of course, the myth is just that — a myth — which enjoys continuing credibility despite the reality of escalating divorce rates, increasing incidences of extramarital affairs, alarmingly high levels of loneliness and despair among both women and men, and numerous media presentations highlighting the wounded and destroyed lives of those suffering domestic violence. Furthermore, the myth allows no room for the reality of long-term, same-sex relationships nor for single or celibate commitments.

While it is true that trust, late childhood friendships, and adolescent socializing are prerequisites to adult relationships, it is erroneous to assume that life-long, meaningful intimacy flows naturally and smoothly from them. Just as individuals do not arrive on the threshold of young adulthood as finished products — mature women and men — neither do relationships happen in finished form just because people have weathered adolescent interactions. The ability to relate to others is, in fact, dependent upon an individual's ability to relate to herself or himself, and as people deepen their self-understanding, so, too, do they broaden their capacity for intimacy.[5] It is only logical, then, that the quality and character of relationships change as people evolve through adult development.

It has been only within the past twenty years or so that developmental psychologists have focused serious attention on human challenge and change beyond the age of 18. Prior to this, behavioral scientists and the general public alike acted as if people underwent substantial amounts of development throughout infancy, childhood, and adolescence, then sort of fell into a protracted period of predictably tedious adulthood during which, so the commonly held belief went, grown-ups fell in love, married, raised children, and worked until they got old and entered the process of inevitable physical and mental decline. The forty or more years of adulthood, apart from old age (formally labelled senescence), was perceived as relatively static.

Adulthood as much more than a holding pattern prior to death was a major breakthrough proclaimed in popular and scientific literature published during the 1970s. People *do* change, adulthood is *not* static, and adults *do* progress in their capacity to learn and to integrate new understandings of themselves in relation to themselves, others, and the world.

Research in adult development is still new, yet preliminary findings suggest that the extended experience of adulthood can be subdivided into discrete subperiods, each with its own interpersonal and intrapersonal tasks. Levinson, for example, subdivides adulthood into four periods, which he labels early (ages 20–40), middle (ages 40–60), late (60–80), and late-late (80+) adulthood, and he maintains that people go through major transitions as they progress from one major subdivision to the next.

Adults deal with the same issues during each transition: vocation, relationships, family, career, prayer, and finances. However, their approaches to them vary qualitatively across the lifespan because of deepening maturity resulting from cumulative experiences. For example, *all* transitional adults question intimacy, but young adults moving into their twenties perceive it very differently than do middle-aged adults moving into their forties. The content — intimacy — remains the same; the form — maturity informed by cumulative life experience — changes. Let's look first at early adulthood relationships.

Early Adulthood

In early adulthood, women and men both focus more on quantity than quality. Having many friends and acquaintances is proof to the young adult that she or he is liked, is acceptable, fostering the illusion that the individual is in control. As a 38-year-old sister noted, "My needs and expectations of friends have changed a lot since I was 30. Part of it is the freedom to allow them to develop as they will instead of thinking I give 100 percent." In their approach to relationship, young adults are more externally than internally referenced in that they tend to look outside themselves for personal validation. This is not to say that they are incapable of meaningful interactions, but to acknowledge that the basis of their interactions is different from that of older adults. Jung maintained that the period of youth, which extends until age 40, is a time when people establish themselves in the world by getting an education, developing a career, and selecting a lifestyle. All of these pursuits demand attention to the actions and reactions of others if the individual is to succeed, so the young adult is, of necessity, more externally than internally referenced.

As they mature, adults learn what does and does not work in relationship as some friendships deepen and others die. Acting out their gender-appropriate roles while trying to understand the place of love in their lives, they are truly mystified when things don't work out as they "should" since they did everything "right" — at least, "right" as far as the cultural script is concerned. Painful though these ruptured relationships are, they remain valuable learning opportunities for assessing one's relational style and quality of interaction. A young order cleric once told me that he was tired of playing the game but never getting anywhere. "I guess I thought I could have something meaningful if I continued in my old school pattern of super stud. What a joke! I'm finally learning that there's a heck of a lot more to relationship than that!"

Some, overwhelmed by the hurt of their failed initial attempts at adult intimacy, conclude it's not worth the pain, time, and energy. They swear off relationships, vowing never to get involved again, as did this 46-year-old sister:

> For years I was a kind of model in the community because of all the work I did and the committees I was on. The truth of it was that I was using the work to avoid people. I'd been badly hurt by a friend I met during graduate school, and decided that maybe the Rule was right. You know, keep it and it will keep you. I was hiding behind the Rule and behind my crazy schedule. I'm only now beginning to crawl out from under.

Others, equally hurt, plunge into new interactions without abandoning old behaviors, and hope that by working harder at what didn't work before, they can have greater success in the future. Finally, there are those who evaluate each failed relationship to determine what they liked and disliked about what happened, how they contributed, and how they might modify future behaviors.[6] "All of living is creating relationships," explained a sister, age 51. "The richness of life comes more from that than from work or study, which — without the relational depths — remain sterile and barren."

As people grow into intimacy, they learn about themselves. They discover that they disclose too little or too much too soon or too late; they spend too much or too little quality time with their partner; they are not mutual enough; they assume too much or too little responsibility for the relationship; they are too physical too soon or not physical enough. Speaking to the issue of learning the role of sexuality in his life, a brother summarized:

> Sexuality used to be a negative thing for me; religious simply did not take part in genital sex. However, a religious renewal program, during which we had presentations on sexuality, and during which I read *The Sexual Celibate*, gave me a fuller understanding of the beauty and complexity of sexuality. My involvement with Marriage Encounter also had the same positive effect on me. Now I view sexuality as an important part of my celibate life. My sexuality can enable me to become a more compassionate, affectionate, loving, and human religious. As a summary, I used to see sexuality as an enemy to a celibate life; now I see it as a friend. (AGE 44)

The point is that people have to learn how to be intimate authentically, and that takes time and experience. A woman religious, aged 50, described her journey:

> I am thirty years as a religious. Most [sexual] involvement was ten years ago. They were part of what I felt was a way of expressing my strong affection for the persons involved. They were never talked about, either with the persons involved or with others. The way I and probably the others chose to get out was just to stop, which we did. Unfortunately, the three people are no longer friends of mine. I feel if we had talked perhaps the friendship would still be alive. I feel the sexual aspect was part of "growing up." I no longer want the sexual part but I would like very much to re-establish the other parts of the friendship.

Growth in intimacy also involves challenge and risk, because unsatisfying relationships hurt. It hurts to trust another, only to discover that the other doesn't really care; to risk physical involvement with the expectation of love and respect, only to learn that the other interpreted your vulnerability as a conquest; to invest years in another, only to find out you both are mired in mutual dependency. As a 37-year-old woman religious filled in the questionnaire and realized that her best friend, a male she had known for more than twenty years, had not been as invested in her as she was in him, she wrote, "I wonder if this relationship would have been better if we had had sex?" What her question reveals is a profound hurt of disappointment and the wistful wondering, couched in the cultural "given" that women must play at sex in order to get love, that he might have been more responsive to her if she had only met his sexual needs. Fortunately, this woman was able to see the relationship for what it was and had the courage to pursue new friendships rather than to torture herself with frustration or personal compromise.

Early adulthood, then, is a time of relational exploration and experimentation during which cultural myths and stereotypes about sexuality, relationships, and intimacy are challenged, questioned, and, sometimes, shattered. As if the pain and exhilaration of intimacy in young adulthood were not enough, the relational plot thickens for people even more as they move into midlife transition and embark upon their interiorization process, a major component of which is re-evaluation of the role of relationship in their lives.[7]

Midlife Transition and Intimacy, Sexuality, and Celibacy

By the time most people arrive at their midlife transition, they have experienced almost twenty years' worth of adult living. Careers have been explored, family constellations have shifted, self-knowledge has emerged, and relationships have been celebrated and mourned. Busy with their "projects" of proving themselves in the world (in the Jungian sense), most men and women in early adulthood employed the skills and attitudes promulgated by society as appropriate to their gender for establishing their niches in adult groups, and begin to doubt, as part of their midlife transitions, if that's all there is. Men who have achieved independence wonder if their hard-won autonomy is worth the loneliness they feel; women who have woven their web of relationships wonder if their interactions with others have been purchased at the expense of their own identity. Especially in the relational arena, women and men begin to eye each other's world in a "grass is greener" context, so men envy women's ability to be intimate with a best friend while women envy men's freedom and self-assuredness. Both sexes start to re-evaluate the truth of what they learned about life when the old answers no longer work for the new questions.

The major task of midlife transition is to develop an internal frame of reference, a personal philosophy of life rooted in self-understanding and self-acceptance that will direct the person through the second half of her or his life.[8] Interiorization, the actual process of entering into the self to review and revise earlier self-understanding and self-definitions, takes several years and is seldom comfortable because it shakes people to their core during a time when, they are convinced, they can least afford the time.[9] Many report feeling as if they are going crazy because they are so flooded with self-doubt and uncertainty. Appearing to be doing well on the outside, seemingly settled in vocations, careers, and relationships they have worked on for nearly two decades, they report feeling chaotic on the inside because they question the extent to which they are truly committed to those very same external realities.

Searching to figure out who they really are, transitional adults question their earlier philosophies of life, wondering why they opted for their given career, lifestyle, or relational commitment. Even more traumatic for some, they wonder why they stay in these commitments. One 53-year-old sister expressed this dilemma:

> A few times in my religious life I have longed to be sexually intimate with a special male friend or wanted marriage, but, for the most part, I have been content to be "appropriately affectionate." If I had to relive my life, however, I'm not certain I would choose celibacy again.

What many transitional adults discover as they pursue their interiorization process is that their earlier commitments were often a living out of others' expectations rather than personal, internally rooted aspiration. For example, some find themselves in education only to admit, after twenty years, that they really do not like it but that they did it because their parents or their congregation wanted them to. Others find themselves in long-term commitments that were "programmed" for them by family or circumstances.

While reviewing commitments made at a younger age, transitional adults are simultaneously questioning their own understandings of their personal identities. They wonder who they are, what they are about, and where they want to go; they ponder ultimate issues, asking themselves who they would die for and what they would live for. It is through immersing themselves in such profound questions that transitional women and men take a serious adult look at their lives and realize, often for the first time, that they have never really taken time to perceive themselves as responsible to themselves rather than as young people responding to external pressures.

Much of what I have been saying and will continue to say about midlife transition for the next few pages I have said before in *Midlife Wanderer* and has been documented by others in the field. I repeat it here, not to be tedious, but to situate the shifts in relational experience as it emerges during this unique period of adult development. Adult transitions are relational transitions, a point that cannot be overstated yet is too often overlooked. Those familiar with adult transition material may want to skip over the next few paragraphs; those unfamiliar with it, or those desiring a brief refresher course, might find the following pages helpful in appreciating the context of emerging intimacy needs.

Today's middle-aged vowed celibates had no role models for weathering the turmoils of transition because their parents or the older members of the congregation, if they went through such a process, did not talk about it. In this respect, adult transitions are both culture- and time-bound. For example, today's middle-aged adults had parents who grew up in a world that expected one career, one vocation, and one family per lifetime; it was a world where commitments were forever, even if that meant deadening adherence to work or relationships impulsively undertaken at too young an age. Such tenacity was rooted in the cultural myth of the time that the world was predictable, rules were inviolable, and steadfastness, regardless of the cost, was virtuous.

Contemporary middle-agers grew up in a very different world. On the one hand, they were promised the stability of their parents' Church and culture, but on the other hand, they matured into early adulthood experiencing the reality of political, economic, ecclesiastical, and personal chaos. Their promised future of trust and respect if only they followed the rules shattered under the upheaval of international intrigue, Vatican II, humanistic psychology, and the sexual and gender revolutions. Their tools for coping and surviving, taught them in their youth, simply did not sustain them. All these external, culturally rooted changes contributed to the intensity of the internal, and until recently, unexamined predictable experience of midlife transition, the protracted period of self-doubt, self-questioning, and personal re-evaluation during which each adult struggles to identify a personal philosophy of life strong enough to motivate and direct the second half of life.

To deal with these questions, transitional adults, especially those in midlife transition, begin to acknowledge that the hard and fast categorizations of their youth are inadequate for containing the realities of their age; they see that there are more areas of gray than of black and white. From the vantage point of their own lived experience, they affirm that morality can be relative, commitments can be both valid and temporary, careers change, and relational needs shift. Questioning what they did wrong to bring them to such ambiguity, suspecting a cause-effect link between past transgressions and current discomfort, they discover that there are no reasons good enough to account for their conundrum. Trapped in tension between what was and what is yet to be, they find themselves in unfamiliar territory. It is as if they recognize the scenery but can't locate the familiar landmarks.

Fragmentation is total, pervading every aspect of their being. They struggle to assess where and how they fit in their families, ministries, congregations, and friendship networks. They question God, prayer, and spirituality. Their previously defined roles, complete with clearly articulated expectations and boundaries, are suddenly more amorphous, fuzzy, than ever before. Some of their questions: How can I function as a grateful daughter or son to my aging parents who need my help more than I need theirs? How can I be a productive and effective administrator to people who held the position before I took over? How can I profess "party line" faith and values when I'm not sure I believe in them myself? What does it mean to be a vowed celibate today, especially when nobody I trust seems to have the answers? Just what *is* intimacy, and how does it fit into my understanding of myself as a woman or man in a vowed celibate commitment? How do I establish appropriate boundaries for touch and affection? All these questions pivot on the same basic query: Who do I say I am, and how do I live that out honestly?

To answer this, transitional adults must relinquish the security of externally imposed parameters of personal identity and enter into the frightening and freeing realm of essential aloneness, that scary and sacred space within the human condition where all people, no matter how close they are to another, stand ultimately separate from others, naked before self and, ultimately, Whomever or Whatever they call God. In essential aloneness we confront the unbridgeable chasm that exists between us and everybody else, thus hurling us into the tragedy of the incomplete human condition and the tremendous restlessness of the human spirit in search of connectedness and truth. Only through surrendering all previous false securities of an externally defined self can each of us begin to see ourselves as we truly are in our powerlessness as well as our potential.

Ruthless though such nakedness seems, especially at first, it is essentially the vehicle to greater wholeness and fullness of life, the opportunity to see and embrace ourselves as we are rather than as what others say we should be. To identify and to claim ourselves from that deepest place within, what some call our heart of hearts, is to free ourselves from the artificially imposed restraints of culturally sanctioned roles and behaviors generated to perpetuate the status quo while simultaneously diminishing persons by restricting their total human expression — their sexuality, which is the physical manifestation of their spirituality.

At the risk of understatement, midlife transition with its concomitant interiorization and existential aloneness is no easy task. It demands a brutal honesty that, though painful, is liberating; it allows, even demands, that we grow up to ourselves, which in turn affects our presence to others.

Adult transitions are, then, relational transitions through which adults re-evaluate their relationships to themselves, others, and God. Thus, relationship is *the* watershed issue of adult transition. Speaking directly to this in the context of her celibate commitment, a sister, aged 37, wrote, "For me, I'm only beginning to know celibacy. Since I've begun the midlife journey into identity and my own sexuality, I can appreciate the choice I've made and hope that celibacy can be optional for those of us in religious life in the future."

The transitional man, eye to eye with himself and painfully lonely and alone, asks why he has to be so autonomous, self-assured, and in control. "Who ever said," he questions, "that I'm not permitted to be vulnerable, gentle, or nurturing? So what if I've made it to the top? What difference does it make if the paycheck, director's position, or principalship leave me feeling so empty?" Such queries precipitate gruelling analyses of the validity of the male system and frequently lead to rejection of its myths, thus freeing him to pursue meaningful, in-depth relationships with women and men alike. It releases him from the cultural bonds that precluded self-disclosure, even if he is unsure of how to proceed in relational risk. He is free to claim himself as person rather than as a caricature of cultural expectation. An order cleric, 49 years old, explained, "Emotional and physical closeness takes the dullness out of life for me. It also energizes me like nothing else. I keep telling my female friend I don't know what or how I'd make it through life without her."

The transitional woman, naked before herself and painfully lonely and alone, asks why she has to be so nurturing, supportive, and involved. She raises her own set of questions: "Whoever said that others always come first while I come last? Who determined that I am worthwhile only when I am doing something for others? Why can't I feel more confident and competent within myself about the things that are important to me?" Her investigations precipitate analyses of her cultural myths and free her to claim herself as a person rooted in herself.

For both, adult midlife transition is the opportunity to break open the truths of their lives while they claim themselves as total persons. Giving themselves permission to challenge what they have learned about women and men, intimacy, sexuality, and celibacy, they allow themselves to fashion personal understandings of these from the sacred spaces within themselves. As a 49-year-old sister asked, "Sexual activity in the vowed life proposes many difficulties, but if the love is truly sincere and growthful, does it not have a place?" Through transition, men become less fearful of intimacy and women become less fearful of sexuality; both become more open to viewing *all* aspects of growth and development as process rather than the product they were taught in their youth. Adults who embrace the dark night of transition report a new freedom in their relationships, one grounded in exciting depths of interaction and meaningful self-expression. "It was so wonderful to be so totally accepted and loved," wrote a woman religious, age 50. "It was easy to get genitally involved. After many years of guilt over this behavior versus the vowed life, we broke with that part of the relationship and have remained best friends."

It is possible that a person is unable or unwilling to suffer the journey; after all, the security of predetermined, externally imposed guidelines and limits is very attractive to someone in turmoil. In these cases, women and men move into chronological midlife while remaining in psychological adolescence or early adulthood. The rigidity with which they adhere to cultural mandates regarding acceptable behavioral parameters is directly proportional to the depth of their fear of ambiguity and change.

Successfully negotiating adult transition, particularly in midlife, does not guarantee quality intimacy and authentic, well integrated sexuality; it does, however, give adults permission to begin to work toward them. And the process of developing meaningful understandings of relationships, sexuality, and celibacy is precisely that: a process. It takes time and energy to allow the self to emerge, which, in turn, requires a toleration of suspended certainty.

Intimacy, sexuality, and celibacy as process reflect a female system approach to human development whereas the same issues approached as product is more male system. Neither embraces the totality of reality, and each demands the other for direction and balance. People need to have a sense of what sexuality is (product) so that they can identify and grow into it through their lived experiences and ever-changing self-understanding (process). Too much product begets stagnating rigidity; too much process, chaotic anarchy.

Middle-aged vowed celibates learned much about intimacy, sexuality, and celibacy as product, concepts with clearly defined boundaries and concrete limits of behaviors within those boundaries. It seems that psychologically androgynous vowed women and many psychologically feminine men are searching to incorporate a process, female system understanding as well. In a recent article entitled "Lesbian Nuns and Midlife Transition," Jeannine

Gramick proposed the shape of what this shift would look like in terms of perceiving celibacy:

> I find that lesbian religious, particularly those in the middle years, are rejecting this traditional approach to celibacy and intimacy in favor of an alternative interpretation. They believe that celibacy, to be authentically human, must maximize opportunities for developing close, intimate relationships. This conception of celibacy springs from women's strong inclinations for relatedness and connection. This new, woman-centered construction of celibacy is marked by caring, friendship and responsibility.... A viable ethic for a woman-defined celibacy includes personal integrity, mutuality, cooperation, responsibility and interdependence rather than fulfillment of an obligation or adherence to a sexual rule. The self and the other are treated with equal value and worth despite, at times, certain difficulties in personal or structural power. Although exclusion may be necessary sometimes, this vision of celibacy and intimacy strives to include all. Lesbian nuns in their middle years are beginning to rethink celibacy in these more inclusive and integration terms.[10]

My contacts with vowed celibates of both sexes, as well as results from my research, suggest that lesbian nuns are not alone in their midlife efforts and that Gramick's comments are applicable to many — gay, straight, and ambisexual — engaged in the journey.

Summary

All living is growing, and neither life nor growth ceases at age 21. Recent advances in the behavioral sciences have explored the dynamics of adult development and have identified predictable periods of challenge and change, all of which have the potential to refine attitudes and behaviors regarding relationships and intimacy, as people mature through the life cycle.

During early adulthood, women and men behave out of culturally mandated scripts of masculine and feminine interaction. For both, the emphasis is on quantity more than quality. Some interactions succeed and others fail as they experiment with their interpersonal skills, and though these experiences might be frustrating or guilt provoking, they are essential to the relational growth process.

As part of midlife transition, and later in preretirement and retirement transition, adults move into a whole new perception of themselves that challenges much of what they were taught earlier in life. They question the limits of their identity and formulate authentic avenues of self-expression consistent with their deepest understanding of themselves as they give themselves permission to explore relationships, sexuality, and celibacy in ways they never dreamed possible in their initial formation. In short, they begin to see life, in all its kaleidoscopic dimensions, more as process and less as product. Just as humans are beings in the process of becoming, so too are their human endeavors, including their intimacies, sexuality, and celibacy. All are predictable changes in the adult developmental spiral toward greater fullness in truth.

Chapter 6

RELATIONAL EMERGENCE OVER TIME

It's been interesting to go through this [questionnaire]. Got me to think a lot. I realize that I've been through a lot of growth in this area. In my younger days, I didn't have any close friends but lots of acquaintances. In a way, I was a model religious. Then, through lots of experiences, some good and some pretty awful, I came to see that relationships are a two-way street and take time. I'm really blessed to have a best friend now, a guy I worked with years ago who is still a good friend. I've never violated celibacy, and I still get curious. I know I've got more to learn, but everything has been worth it. (BROTHER, AGE 54)

Mine is a sordid story; thank God this is anonymous! Looking back, I can see how naive I was. Yes, I got pregnant, and thought it would never happen to me. I've never been more frightened, humiliated. I did the only thing I could at the time — I had an abortion. As far as I know, nobody knows about this. I thought he loved me, but that was a joke. As soon as the pregnancy was "taken care of," he was gone. To think that I fell for all those old lines about love and sex. I've grown through my mistakes, even though I'm not proud of myself. Go ahead and tell my story if you want, especially if you think it will help anyone else. (SISTER, AGE 47)

What a gift friendship has been for me. Without it, I don't think I could stay in the order and active ministry. She has given me such life and love. It's been hard, and I had to learn to open up and be more available. I wish I could have learned some of this earlier, but maybe it was all part of growing up. (DIOCESAN PRIEST, AGE 38)

The piece that was my breakthrough in all this was identifying my sexual orientation. I'd been attracted to both men and women, and thought I was weird because of it. So, to protect myself, I kept distant from everybody. It took lots of reading and a few workshops, but I finally learned about bisexual women — what I think I am, and found out that others were the same way. There was something settling in that. Anyhow, once I could accept myself for me, I just felt freer to trust more. Now I have two wonderful friendships, one with a man and one with a woman. I'm affectionate with both. (SISTER, AGE 44)

Evidence from the material so far indicates that vowed women and men value relationship, that many have engaged in some degree of sexual expression, and that the majority endorse a "personal investment" approach to celibacy. No one explanation exists to clarify these phenomena.

Behavioral science literature suggests that women and men grow into deeper intimacy and more rewarding interpersonal interactions as they mature into adulthood and develop an internally referenced philosophy of life. The more integrated people become, the more they seek interactions with others who have also claimed, or are searching for, an authentic identity. From a developmental perspective, then, it is not surprising that middle-aged vowed celibates prioritize the role of relationships in their lives. Even though they were brought up in a culture and Church of sexual denial and were discouraged from developing close friendships as part of their formation training, they indicate that they have made decisions about themselves and the place of relationships and sexuality in their lives that suggest openness to a growth process unavailable to them in early adulthood.

The whys and hows of this journey are unclear. Perhaps some vowed celibates embrace intimacy as essential to their lives because they have weathered the unpredictabilities of adult development and have arrived at an understanding of themselves that is different from the externally endorsed identity of their youth. Perhaps they pursue intimacy because, as a group, they transcend stereotypic guidelines for gender-appropriate behaviors. Some may have grown into appreciation of intimacy because of community living, where proximity and shared values of lifestyle and faith contributed some common bases of attraction and interaction. Others, pressured by the sexual revolution of the culture combined with the loneliness inherent in *any* lifestyle, may have pursued relationship and/or sexuality in hopes of a quick fix of instant intimacy. Whatever the underpinnings of their current values and beliefs, vowed celibates are quite clear on one thing: the journey is not easy.

Detours along the Relational Path

Many report that their affectional and sexual interactions were deliberately chosen and mutually decided upon, but not all were clear or comfortable. It is naive to assume that all vowed celibates enjoy marvelously enriching intimacies or that they somehow magically arrived at fulfilling relationships because of the *Bem* scores or their midlife transitions. Learning to relate meaningfully takes time, energy, and motivation; people have fluctuating reserves of these as they juggle ministerial responsibilities, familial demands, and adult developmental processes.

It is also important to remember that middle-aged adults, whether vowed celibates or not, grew up during a time when sex and sexuality were largely verboten topics, and early trainings die hard. In other words, the most sophisticated intellectual understanding of sexuality as total human expression can be seriously undermined by a childhood fear of sex as dirty and sinful that impedes even the most cursory overture of friendship toward another. Many vowed celibates report that their early childhood "tapes" are the major obstacle to their adult relational efforts. Superstitions and threats taught us in youth have an irrationally powerful hold because they were predicated upon instilling fear at a time when we had neither the cognitive maturity nor life experiences to challenge or balance them. Some try to work this through with friends, personal reading, human sexuality workshops, and counseling or spiritual direction. Others struggle quietly and alone. For all, questioning, reassessing, and reversing early messages is a life-long endeavor, and even those who report long-standing best friendships of ten years' duration or longer complain of unwelcomed nagging doubts about the appropriateness of their intimacy within the context of vowed celibate community living intended for apostolic availability.

Many vowed celibates admit to a type of "relational baptism by fire" wherein they've learned more of what *not* to do to be intimate or of what does *not* constitute intimacy because of their series of misadventures and "mistakes." For example, recall the sister quoted earlier who thought she was safe from any sexual concerns because she had vowed celibacy. Her own naiveté took her by surprise and, while undoubtedly painful for her, taught her some important things about herself as a person in relationship and as a physical woman. "I should have known better than to sit in front of the fire with him at that hour of the night!" or "I was crazy to visit her alone in her house!" are variations on the same theme — naiveté. Mistakes resulting from naiveté are particularly painful, because we all pride ourselves on being intelligent and circumspect and somehow above what we perceive to be "adolescent flounderings." Ignorance may not be an acceptable excuse for some, but it still hurts. Those who have been burned because of their naiveté recover best when they can talk about what they have been through because they are freed from carrying their burden alone.

Some, inexperienced with alcohol or drugs, confused chemical "high" with emotional involvement. Others were genitally active while intoxicated, and some had little or no memory of the event as a result. An exhaustive review of the interaction of substance abuse or addiction and sexuality is beyond the scope of this discussion. While overly simplistic, sufficient for now is this observation: Some suffer sexuality difficulties because they have abuse or addiction problems; other have substance abuse problems because they have unresolved sexuality issues. Each contributes to and exacerbates the other. The fact remains that some vowed celibates have said or done things under the influence of drugs or alcohol that they later regret.

Products of the culture, including the media's indoctrination that romantic, soap opera love complete with genital activity is the ultimate expression of intimacy (the male system definition), some became physically involved because they assumed it was part of the adult interaction script. Her "I thought it was what he wanted" is regrettably the refrain to his, "I thought it was what she expected!" In these instances, both parties ended up victims of covert coercion, misunderstanding, and miscommunication.

Curiosity is another culprit in the litany of relational casualties, and given the pervasiveness of sexual taboos from their youth and early adulthood, middle-aged vowed celibates were and are particularly vulnerable to it. "What's so awful about a particular friendship that I should avoid it at all costs?" is a predictable question, as is the rationalization, "Sex must be pretty wonderful if it's the one thing I can't do!" By their very repression, both particular friendships and sex become preoccupations — events to be experienced for their own sake — and vowed celibates often pursued them with the fervor of women and men with a mission, bent on their task of tasting the forbidden fruits lest they die denied these penultimate experiences. Curiosity magnifies and exaggerates. Of course, quality sex education and open discussion would do much to alleviate the obsession, but neither was available to the majority of vowed celibates during their formation and early adulthood. Even as adults, most vowed celibates are uncomfortable discussing sexuality concerns.

Some responded to the passion of the moment, like the 44-year-old cleric who wrote that two of his sexual encounters with men were clearly reactions to "raging hormones." Others, suffering from physical and/or emotional exhaustion, were vulnerable in ways they could not have anticipated because they had never been in those situations before and did not have the resources to cope. Had they been better rested or more experienced in decision making while in a compromised condition, they might have responded very differently.

Some misinterpreted infatuation or the emotional high of a new relationship as true love and engaged in physical behaviors they might ordinarily not allow. In these instances, events tended to unfold rapidly, as if they had a life of their own, which, in infatuation, is true. The pain remaining once the infatuation has run its course is tremendous, and the embarrassment is generally great. Vowed celibates will repeat "infatuation mistakes" unless they learn to name what they have been through so they are better prepared to deal with it in the future — because they will be infatuated again!

Identifying boundaries or limits is a life-long task, and every interpersonal success or failure presents another learning opportunity. For instance, some say, "I have learned that it is not very wise for me to be alone late at night with a friend I find sexually attractive when we are both tired and lonely, but that it is perfectly okay and comfortable for me to seek this person's company during the day in a public place." Likewise, "Through the trial and error of relational growth, I've discovered that I'm the type of person who has to proceed slowly with new friends because I've identified a tendency in myself to overinvest too soon as a result of the emotional high I feel during the initial stages of a new relationship." In a third scenario, "I've learned that unless I question my motivations regularly and honestly, I have a pattern of passive-aggressive responses that can kill a relationship."

There is no predetermined time sequence for growth in intimacy; people learn when they are ready. Some older sisters demonstrated this during a workshop years ago when one 72-year-old woman expressed her chagrin over feeling left out by changes in the relational rules of religious life. "For years," she said, "I stayed away from particular friendships because that's the way it was. I was attracted to many different people, but I kept distant. Now you're telling me I *should* have a best friend. That makes me mad, because all those I wanted for a best friend have either left the community or have died. What am I supposed to do?"

"Oh, stop your complaining," another elderly sister admonished. "You ain't dead yet, honey! Go find somebody else!"

Excursions into the mysteries of relational growth can be rocky, as a 52-year-old diocesan priest describes:

> I went through twenty years of confusion, denial, rationalization and determined suppression of sexual feelings. It was only through a couple of "breaks" in my early to middle thirties that I finally got to "deal with" my physical, emotional, sexual, relational life. I think I'm still learning that the same human person can be both spiritual and sexual, both intellectual and emotional. I'm beginning to think that a *healthy physical life* helps to resolve those polar opposites, or at least to get them on talking terms. I think I'm also beginning to get over my disrespect and dislike for sex as though it's the greatest trouble-maker in life. But then I've made the mistake of premature resolutions before. Whatever it is I'm learning,

and whatever it is I'm becoming — is at least something I trust — and look forward to! "Spouse of Christ" may sound corny, pretentious, or outdated theologically, but a personal and gradually realized relationship with God in Christ and Christ in the human sphere of life is what I think my celibate life and (sometimes comic) struggles are all about.

Another variable to be factored into the current discussion is the impact of being an adult survivor of a dysfunctional family pattern on the ability to develop and sustain intimacy.

I'm 57 years old. I'm on sabbatical for this year. I got into counseling and found I have some dysfunctional family background that I was not aware of. Most of this dysfunctional past was in the area of intimacy. I also came through a pre–Vatican II religious life training. Now at this age I find that intimacy is very important for growth and wholistic living. As I look back I did have a best friend only in the last few years. But I think I was holding back or I could say afraid of close friendship and intimacy. After this counseling and sabbatical time, I look at intimacy a lot differently and hope to pursue this friendship further. I hope and pray I'm ready.
(BROTHER, AGE 57)

While there are many forms of dysfunctional families, the two most extensively researched today are alcoholic families and incestuous families. As Sean Sammon reports in his recent text, *Alcoholism's Children: ACoAs in Priesthood and Religious Life*, people who grew up in alcoholic families learned ways of behaving that mitigate against the formation of healthy intimacy; they have not experienced the parenting and personal recognition that are prerequisites of strong ego development necessary for the give-and-take of mature adult relationships.[1] Their roles as heroes, invisible children, and jokesters, among others, override their identities as persons. Until they recognize, accept, and move beyond their role entrapments, they are not really free to pursue adult intimacy.

Adult survivors of sexual abuse also experience difficulties with relationships. Current research reports that between 25 and 34 percent of all females and one in seven males are adult survivors,[2] and that as many as 50 percent of women religious are adult survivors.[3] These people are in double jeopardy in the relational arena: (1) they have been robbed of their ability to trust because of the role violation perpetrated by their abusers and (2) they have been taught distorted lessons about their sexuality and its role in their lives. To complicate matters, many adult survivors enter ministry and vow celibacy with no conscious memories of their abuse. It is not until they work through their childhood trauma that they can even begin to deal with intimacy and sexuality issues in an honest way as adults.[4]

ACoAs and adult survivors both have access to support groups and treatment programs unavailable to earlier generations, and many are making use of them. Unfortunately, some people do not even know that their childhoods were atypical, erroneously assume that everyone grew up in comparable home environments, and unconsciously perseverate in unproductive relationships with inadequate or self-defeating interaction patterns. As ACoA and adult survivor literature proliferates, more people will have the opportunity to address their issues and makes choices for change. The truth for all of us, whether ACoAs or adult survivors, is that we are products of our past, but we do not have to be victims to our future.

How might adult survivor status affect the numbers of women religious claiming heterosexual, lesbian, or ambisexual identities? What about the men? Is there any relationship between adult survivor status and affectional/sexual experiences among vowed celibates? What impact, if any, would adult survivor or ACoA status have on claiming a best friend? Results of my research are inadequate for answering these questions, but future investigations can take a more in-depth look at the issues.

Despite the early conditioning, confusions, problems, setbacks, errors in judgment, adult survivor status, raging hormones, exhaustion, or naiveté, many middle-aged vowed celibates seem willing to remain engaged in the struggle toward authentic intimacy. Others, paralyzed by or guilt-ridden over their "baptism by fire," opt out of the relational arena, concluding it is simply too much for them to handle within the limits of their self-definitions as persons and as vowed celibates. Some, fearful of making mistakes, never enter the relational ring at all; they settle for lives that are celibately correct but interpersonally sterile. Others may find themselves endorsing all three stances at one time or another, depending upon where they are intra- and interpersonally at various points along their developmental path.

As I've said all along, there is no single sequence nor predetermined pattern of growth in relationship. All do the best they can with what they've got, and make new decisions when they get new information. What *does* seem unique to vowed celibates in general is their conscious commitment to understanding and pursuing intimacy that is countercultural both to the prevailing male system and to their early training in religious and clerical life. Because they have virtually no role models for their endeavors as vowed celibates, they are courageous anomalies in a world that craves security and certainty, even at the expense of personal freedom. Their efforts may win them ridicule or kudos — only the future will tell.

Personal and Psychotherapeutic Considerations

Nothing develops in a vacuum, and celibate sexual intimacy is no exception. To live, to grow, and to err are all fine hypothetically, but there comes a point when personal process butts up against harsh reality. Based on my therapeutic and educational encounters with priests, sisters, and brothers, I'd like to offer a few comments to vowed celibates and those who work with them in counseling. First, I'd like to list some of the things vowed celibates have told me they have found helpful in their relational development, then discuss each one in detail. The list is not exhaustive; please add to, challenge, or refute what I propose.

1. Identify early messages about relationship, sexuality, and celibacy, and try to decide which are valid and invalid for you today.

2. Write out your relational/sexual/celibate history, and see if you can identify patterns. What do these tell you, both positively and negatively, about yourself?

3. Where do your romantic notions about relationship enhance or diminish your ability to relate?

4. How might early familial interactions, roles, and myths have an impact on your current relationships?

5. What do you know about sex, sexuality, intimacy, and celibacy? What do you need to learn about these to free yourself in relationship?

6. What is your sexual orientation? What do you know about it and how comfortable are you with it?

7. What are your limits or boundaries regarding touch, affection, time, and place with those you love? What are your signals, and how do you respond to them?

8. To what extent do your personal behaviors court accusations of scandal? How familiar and comfortable are you with the ethics of your local community, and how willing are you to respect and accommodate them?

9. Where do you locate yourself in your adult developmental process, and what does this mean to you in terms of what you are thinking, feeling, and doing?

10. How honest are you being with yourself, others, and God about what you are doing and why?

Hardly comprehensive, this brief list begins to reflect some of the concerns I hear from vowed celibates in workshops, renewal programs, and private counseling. They all boil down to the same fundamental question: How well do I know myself, and what am I willing to do about what I know?

The first item addresses our personal childhood experiences of intimacy and sexuality, something that "happened to us" without our permission but from which we operate, often unconsciously, for the rest of our lives. For example, many grew up in homes where the never articulated but strongly felt ethic of "Put up, shut up, and offer it up" reigned supreme. Discussions of sex and intimacy were not overtly forbidden, but stiffened backs and tolerant smiles when the topics were raised clearly conveyed the message that they were "not okay" subjects to talk about. Additionally, excessive secrecy or joking about sex, menstruation, nocturnal emissions, or personal anatomy were indications that some issues were better left unsaid. To be able to describe and name these early lessons are valuable keys to unlocking the wordless chains that imprison our sexual selves. Everyone has a story, but not everyone knows it. Needing to preserve our myths about perfect parents, some of us cannot even begin to name the reality of our early sexual environment, regardless of its deleterious effect on our adult sexual adjustment. In the words of a 54-year-old sister:

> Ours was a sexually informed but repressed family. As kids, we knew all the anatomy and physiology of puberty and sex. But that was the lie! We were allowed to talk about it, even tease about it, but we weren't *ever* to experience or feel it. I can talk intimacy up one side and down the other, but I feel dirty and bad if I experience it myself. It's as if I'd betray my virtue — and my parents!

To name, claim, and reframe the early tapes is to gift ourselves with the freedom to make adult decisions about adult relationships. Our parents were neither ignorant nor malicious, and they did the best they could with what they had. It's just that some of us had parents who were uninformed about or uncomfortable with sex and who passed on the prejudices they learned from *their* parents.

The early childhood lessons are more than sex messages, of course. They include formidable information about how men and women interact, how they tease, and what they can or cannot do in the presence of another. To decode their messages is to claim adult choice — and responsibility. This is a vital but frequently ignored piece of our adult sexuality. For some, it is easier to blame Mom and Dad than it is to deal with personal growth demands.

Writing one's relational history is both freeing and frightening, because it brings us into the stark reality of our own interpersonal imperfections as well as the painful insight that we too often fail to learn from our own mistakes. To admit that we pursue only safe partners, those who, because of other life commitments, are not free to commit to us, is to acknowledge that we unwittingly set ourselves up to be disappointed and to rationalize that the other person is the source of our disappointment and frustration. Discovering that we are consistently dependent or overbearing, that we stay with someone until we are genital together, or that we remain only superficially engaged, is to learn something vital about ourselves in relationship and to face the choice to change.

Each of us carries childhood fairy tale fantasies into our adult interactions without necessarily realizing the unrealistic expectations of our romantic notions. Beliefs that there is one and only one person "out there" for us, that love is eternal bliss, that our partners can read our minds and meet all our needs, that true intimacy is effortless, or that real friendship means we never argue or disagree are alluring and even fun, but also dangerous and guaranteed to disappoint. They may work in the movies or on TV, but are superficial and false in our daily relational struggles. Romeo and Juliet are an attractive couple whose tragic demise we too often forget. Intimate relationships have many wonderful romantic moments, but romance alone cannot sustain relationships. Unfortunately, our culture's addiction to romance obfuscates recognizing and working at real intimacy.

Every family has a myth — a story — in which we assumed or were assigned roles that can unconsciously dictate adult interactions. Playing the buffoon, hard guy, Casanova, femme fatale, rescuer, or peacemaker may have helped us to survive and even enjoy childhood, but can be lethal in restricting our adult repertoire of relational skills and sensitivities. Positive and productive relationships are beyond our reach until we can free ourselves of our assigned interactional roles. A diocesan priest told his story:

> It wasn't until my early fifties that I finally saw the connection between my "strong, silent male role" and my inability to be intimate. My family relied on me to absorb all the pain that came our way, including my father's disability and my mother's inadequacy, and I played it out perfectly. Only last year did I finally see that I didn't have to take it on the chin, and realized that my life was a pattern of seeking out troubled people who needed a sounding board. I was never really free to be myself. (AGE 56)

Some learn to identify their childhood roles through dialogue with family members, some work them through alone, and others explore them with friends or professionals. The "how" of naming our roles is not as important as the hard work of choosing change once the roles or myths are articulated. This is one area in which ACoA literature has been invaluable to many; it names and describes many of the dysfunctional family's roles that carry over into adulthood.

I repeatedly meet adult vowed celibates who have a dearth of solid sex education background. Women and men with doctorates in esoteric disciplines, renowned in their fields, often lack the most basic information about their bodies and their human sexual response. Predictably, their limited sex education is accompanied by an irrational suspicion of relationship and a fear-based theology of celibacy. There are, fortunately, numerous programs providing both didactic information and values exploration components available throughout the U.S. and Canada at schools, renewal centers, and through congregational and diocesan in-service programs. Giving ourselves permission to admit that we don't know everything or that we might benefit from a refresher course is to gift ourselves with freedom for greater growth in relationship. Additionally, most of the adult ed sexuality programs are specifically designed to help participants explore their attitudes about their sexuality and to encourage them to deal with their values and fears surrounding sexuality. Many have told me that participation in such a program was the first time they ever had the opportunity to talk about sex in such an open forum and to discover that they were not alone in their feelings.

Whether genitally active or not, we possess and act out of a sexual orientation, be that straight, gay, or ambisexual. To identify our orientation and to embrace it as an integral aspect of our sexuality is essential for both personal peace and honesty. Readings, support groups, and educational programs are all available to facilitate this process. To conclude, "I don't need to worry about sexual orientation because I'm celibate" is to beg the question and to live a lie since our ability to be comfortable with others' orientation is dependent upon our ability to be comfortable with our own. This does not mean that we necessarily have to proclaim our orientation to the entire world to be "real"; that could be meaningless and counterproductive to many ministers and those to whom they minister. It *does* demand a personal honesty, however, which we may or may not choose to share with others.

Learning our genital and affectional boundaries is a life-long task encompassing successes and failures, humor and humiliation. To know our strengths and vulnerabilities is to admit that we have both and that we are responsible for acting on them. It may be easier to ask forgiveness than permission, but ignorance — or the pretense of it — is insufficient excuse over the long haul. We need to be enough in touch with ourselves to respect our personal reactions to various combinations of fatigue, loneliness, touch, intoxication, and "raging hormones," and must accept that our reactions shift over age, place, and space. Few boundaries are forever, few limits are constant over time, and seldom are two people alike in where they draw their lines. The intrapersonal scenery is constantly changing, and we are responsible for recognizing its ever-shifting configurations.

People will think and say what they want about our behaviors, and there isn't much we can do about it. What we *can* control, however, are the choices we make regarding what we do and where we do it. This is an appeal to prudence more than an exhortation to secrecy. Ministers are, like it or not, public figures who must be sensitive to and respectful of the people they serve, even if it imposes inconvenience. We may experience perfect congruence between affectional displays with a loved one and our celibate commitment, yet realistically may have to refrain from dining together regularly in the local restaurant or from strolling arm-in-arm late at night through the town square. I'm not advocating that vowed celibates be prisoners in their own homes, nor that they resort to clandestine meetings in secluded settings, behaviors that could backfire with a vengeance in the long run. It may limp as an analogy, but just as married couples do not exercise their conjugal rights in front of house guests, neither do vowed celibates flaunt their private lives in public places. On this issue, vowed celibates have to pick their battles and accept that there are limits to appropriate place and space for their personal interactions. Refusal to do so may result in others making decisions for them.

Given the recent deluge of research on adult development and adult transitions, middle-aged vowed celibates now have access to valuable information of what they can expect as they mature through the life span and can evaluate their feelings and behaviors accordingly. Locating ourselves in midlife transition, for example, helps us to understand that our vocational doubts and relational dilemmas are not problems to be solved through quick-fix solutions, but processes to be experienced for the sake of greater integration. For some, the information reassures them that they are not crazy; it gives them permission to live with ambiguity and confusion. While it is always possible for people to use adult transition as an "excuse" for inappropriate behavior, it more often happens that they accept the information as corroboration of their own experience, which leads to deeper appreciation of their own and others' relational upheavals.

We are as capable of self-deceit as we are of honesty. Ultimately answerable to ourselves in our heart of hearts, only we can truly know our motivations and personal ethics. Others may offer their observations and opinions, but the final evaluation — short of irrefutable scandal — is ours. We might seem exemplary in our celibate lives, yet know deep within that our interpersonal distancing is fear of intimacy rather than commitment to either ministry or chastity. Likewise, we may look as if we are being kind to another, but may realize we are using the others' vulnerability to indulge our own need for control or experimentation. We cannot be absolutely certain of our motives at all times, but we *can* commit ourselves to an honest search for the truth, which occurs through straightforward dialogue with ourselves, God, and others. As always, we make the best decision we can with the information we have; if we learn something new tomorrow, we make a new decision. To discover that we're playing games, kidding ourselves or deceiving others is to remind ourselves humbly that we're human and always have the opportunity to ask forgiveness and to make changes. Embarrassed? Maybe. Uncomfortable? Probably. But it is only to the extent that we are honest with ourselves that we can be honest in our intimacy with another.

These ruminations result from my years' experience of interacting with vowed celibates striving toward authenticity in their relationships with themselves, others, and God. They have employed one or more of these to help themselves in their journeys. Readers may have other ideas and techniques that work as well or better. The question is not "Which is the best way?" but rather, "What works best for me?" The answer will, undoubtedly, evolve over time.

Occasionally vowed celibates seek professional counseling to help them understand and resolve psychosexual and relational questions. Shopping for and finding the right therapist can be a harrowing experience. I will list some professional and ethical guidelines that I believe mental health providers should honor when working with diocesan clergy and women and men religious. If vowed celibates agree with what I propose, they may want to interview a prospective therapist to determine whether or not this person is someone with whom they want to pursue the therapeutic process.

Counselors and psychologists working with vowed celibates have an ethical obligation to be as familiar as possible with their clientele and their lifestyle to avoid misinformation or naive assumptions about priests, sisters, and brothers. If they are unable to respect or to see the validity of celibate commitments, then they are not in a position to work with this group without doing violence to themselves and their clients. Years ago, for example, a psychologist who had just begun working with his first vowed celibate said to me, "I'm willing to see her, but personally I think the notion of a 42-year-old virgin is stupid!" Needless to say, I never referred another sister to him.

Again consistent with their ethical obligation to be familiar with their clients' concerns, mental health professionals seeing middle-aged vowed celibates should be knowledgeable about and updated in adult developmental psychology, men's and women's sexuality, sexual orientation, relational development, adult survivor and ACoA issues, and sexual addictions. To the extent possible, they should be comfortable with their own sexuality so that they do not project their unresolved issues onto their clients. If they morally cannot accept that vowed celibates might engage in genital activity as part of personal growth and development, then they should make this explicitly known to their clients and should, ethically, offer their clients referrals to other therapists who are morally more comfortable. Likewise, sensing a vested interest in talking clients into or out of ministerial life should be a red flag to therapists that they need to examine their objectivity to determine if they have their clients' best interests — and freedom of choice — at heart.

As always, the therapeutic task is to meet clients where they are and to assist them in self-understanding as they move toward greater growth in integration and insight. Formation programs, seminaries, and spiritual direction are *not* therapy, even though they might contain therapeutic moments. Formation directors, spiritual directors, superiors, and rectors, even if they are licensed counselors, psychologists, or social workers, should *never* conduct psychotherapy with their directees while functioning in their leadership or spiritual direction roles; this is dual relationship and is patently unethical and potentially damaging.

Mental health professionals walking with vowed celibates on their psychosexual journeys must remember that the individual, *not* the individual's superior, bishop, or director, is the client, and they must honor confidentiality unless the client is a physical danger to self or another or is abusing children.

Finally, therapeutic "homework assignments" demanding genital activity with another for "desensitization" or to determine sexual orientation is *never* appropriate or ethical. Vowed celibates encountering such pressure should terminate therapy immediately and report their therapist to appropriate authorities.

Selecting a therapist is a very personal matter. All people, regardless of vocation, work best when they feel safe, heard, accepted, and understood. "To feel safe" is not synonymous with "to feel comfortable." Good counseling often hurts. However, if vowed celibates, as clients, feel they must protect or take care of their counselor, censor their comments, or disguise their issues, then they are not with the right therapist and cannot, without violence to themselves, make progress. In short, if counseling is for you, make sure you get what you pay for, both financially and emotionally.

Celibacy — Process or Product?

Reconciling a process definition of celibacy with a product definition of it as proclaimed by the institutional Church is controversial among ministers today, and another area warranting more in-depth study. Neither approach is superior to the other, and individuals will vacillate between the two while working to ascertain the most authentic personal balance within the self — a balance guaranteed to shift as the woman or man matures into middle age. From a diocesan priest, age 42:

> The Church demands a role-conditioned ego on the issue of celibacy, but offers no consolation for those seriously engaged with a struggle on the issue. The help I got I had to find on my own. Though I am now happy, I deeply feel for those who are not. Though I see no change in my lifetime, I do hope it comes.

A sister, aged 49, wrote, "I believe leaders in religious life and the Church are afraid to study celibacy with a new openness because it might empty out the rectories and convents. Yet, no discussion or exploration continues to ferment many secret lives and liaisons." Another approach to the controversy is that explained by this 39-year-old order priest: "I believe celibacy should be one option for those in ministry. However, I believe those who publicly profess celibacy must honestly live that commitment. And I believe we have to be accountable for our honesty." A woman religious, aged 41, disagrees:

> I publicly professed three vows and, quite frankly, have violated all of them as I've grown into deeper understanding of myself in relation to those vows. What I fail to understand is why no one seems to get upset that I've been self-willed or have found ways to "procure" spending money while they become hysterical over the fact that I've loved deeply and have expressed it physically. Understand, I'm not talking about flaunting any of the vows; I *am* talking about the double standard of being permitted to "grow" into two of them while not being permitted to budge at all in the third.

What is clear from listening to vowed celibates today is that there is no unanimity among them regarding the definition of the vow or regarding the validity of the "vow as process" as opposed to the "vow as product." What *is* clear is that many, women and men alike, embrace personal process within their own developmental journey and grow into greater appreciation of intimacy, sexuality, and celibacy as part of their human emergence. They are willing to embrace the uncertainty of ambiguity, sometimes with guilt and remorse and sometimes with joy and celebration. Their stories are multifaceted and reflective of the upheavals, both culturally and ecclesiastically, of the past twenty-five years. Whatever compliments or criticisms today's middle-aged vowed celibates receive for their efforts, their lives stand as testaments to the restlessness of the human spirit as these courageous women and men persist in their quests for greater honesty in their relationships with themselves, with others, and with their God. Their struggles give witness to Joan Ohanneson's exhortation, "If you don't want to change, then don't pray."[5]

APPENDIXES

Appendix A

COVER LETTER TO
STUDY PARTICIPANTS

June 1989

Dear Study Participant,

Thank you for taking the time to assist in this valuable research on the attitudes toward relationship, celibacy, and sexuality of men and women religious and diocesan clergy. While much has been written recently on how women and men differ in their approaches to these important life issues, nothing has been done directly with men and women religious and diocesan clerics on these important topics.

Attached are two research instruments: (1) The Bem Sex Role Inventory and (2) an extensive questionnaire. The Bem is a self-report inventory of your emotional expressions. There are no right or wrong responses. Please do not leave any items blank. The second instrument is a questionnaire consisting of items exploring attitudes and behaviors toward relationship, sexuality, and celibacy. The items are based on findings currently reported in both popular and scientific literature. Again, there are no right or wrong responses, and I ask that you complete as many items as possible. DO NOT put your name on either instrument — indicate ONLY age and sex.

All data will be treated anonymously. You are invited to write in comments or clarifications wherever you like. Please note the final item on the questionnaire: "May I quote you?" If you give your permission, please know that all quotations will be anonymous. No names will be associated with any of these materials.

This study is endorsed by the Religious Formation Conference and it meets the requirements of the American Psychological Association's ethical guidelines for research with human subjects. It is my intention to seek publication of the findings.

Thanks again for your help in this important project. If you have any questions, please do not hesitate to contact me.

Sincerely,

Sheila Murphy, Ph.D.
Psychologist, Lic. No. 2192

Appendix B

QUESTIONNAIRE

[The numbers reported are percentages. The first number is the percentage for female respondents and the second is for males. Where respondents answered more than one item, thus making computation of statistics erroneous or suspect, no percentages are reported.]

Age _____ Sex _____ Age entered religious life/seminary _____

Status (check only one)

_____ sister _____ diocesan clergy

_____ brother _____ order clergy

Number of years in religious life/diocesan clergy _____

Part I. Relationships

This part of the study asks about "best friends." If you can claim a best friend right now, or have been in a best friendship within the past ten years — even if that relationship is no longer active — then please complete this section. For purposes of this investigation, "best friends" are defined as human persons, not pets, deities, or saints.

1. I have a best friend.
     96.61/88.66 yes   *3.39/11.34* no

(If NO, go to PART II of this questionnaire.)

2. This person is
     21.93/59.30 male   *78.07/40.70* female

3. This person knows that s/he is my best friend.
     84.96/89.53 yes   *.88/1.16* no   *14.16/9.30* unsure

4. This relationship has been going on for (check only ONE)

   6.17/10.47 0–2 yrs.   *11.89/9.30* 3–5 yrs.
   20.70/19.77 5–10 yrs.   *61.23/60.47* more than 10 years

5. I see this person

   18.30/22.09 daily   *20.98/23.26* weekly
   35.27/37.21 monthly   *25.45/17.44* yearly or less

6. I talk with/write to this person

   20.26/27.91 daily   *40.53/38.37* weekly
   29.96/26.74 monthly   *9.25/6.98* yearly or less

7. My best friend is

   8.81/18.60 married   *9.25/13.95* single
   10.57/12.79 diocesan cleric   *.88/2.33* divorced
   54.19/26.74 member of my congr.
   16.30/25.58 member of other congr.

8. I assume/hope that this individual would name ME as her/his best friend.

   76.99/73.26 yes   *6.64/12.79* no   *16.37/13.95* unsure

9. When we get together, this friend and I (check only ONE)

   .44/.00 talk almost exclusively about past time we shared together
   .00/.00 talk mostly about past times and a little of our current lives
   15.11/14.29 talk equally about shared past times and our current lives
   61.78/65.48 talk mostly about current lives and a little of past
   22.67/20.24 talk almost exclusively about our current lives

10. I would say that my best friend knows just about everything about me, even my darkest secrets.

    61.95/70.59 yes   *29.65/24.71* no   *8.41/4.71* unsure

11. I would say that I know just about everything about my best friend, even her/his darkest secrets.

    53.10/61.18 yes   *29.20/25.88* no   *17.70/12.94* unsure

12. When planning time together, I would say that the one who plans the majority of the agenda is

    8.85/7.14 me   *13.72/15.48* my friend
    77.43/77.38 we share this equally

13. The one most likely to initiate our get-togethers is
    22.12/24.10 me   *17.26/13.25* my friend
    60.62/62.65 we share this equally

14. When we are together, the one who does the most talking is
    10.18/5.88 me   *19.91/15.29* my friend
    69.91/78.82 we share equally

15. Check any of the following that you do with your best friend. Place a double check mark before the activity that you share most often with your friend. [Results are for double-checked items.]
    11.43/12.70 paid employment/ministry
    2.86/4.76 support group
    50.86/61.90 private time with just the two of us
    4.00/.00 pray together
    8.57/6.35 vacation
    16.00/11.11 socializing/sports
    6.29/3.17 other (please elaborate)

16. I would say that my best friend knows what my favorite foods are.
    76.11/74.12 yes   *5.75/9.41* no   *18.14/16.47* unsure

17. I would say that I know what my best friend's favorite foods are.
    77.43/76.47 yes   *6.64/7.06* no   *15.93/16.47* unsure

18. I would say that my best friend knows my philosophy of life.
    94.71/96.51 yes   *.44/.00* no   *4.85/3.49* unsure

19. I would say that I know my best friend's philosophy of life.
    93.39/96.51 yes   *.44/.00* no   *6.17/3.49* unsure

20. I would say that my best friend knows where I stand on faith issues.
    94.27/98.84 yes   *.88/1.16* no   *4.85/.00* unsure

21. I would say that I know my best friend's stance on faith issues.
    93.39/97.67 yes   *.44/1.16* no   *6.17/1.16* unsure

22. When planning a trip together, the one who does the most planning is
    15.74/11.25 me   *23.61/17.50* my friend
    60.65/71.25 we provide equal input

23. If I ran into serious difficulty, e.g., lost a job, got arrested, had a death in the family, etc., probably one of the first people I would contact would be my best friend.
    92.07/95.35 yes   *3.96/1.16* no   *3.96/3.49* unsure

24. If my friend ran into similar difficulties, I believe that s/he would probably contact me right away.

    76.65/87.21 yes   *8.37/4.65* no   *14.98/8.14* unsure

25. If I had great news — new job, special award, promotion, won the lottery — one of the first I'd contact would be my friend.

    92.51/94.19 yes   *3.08/2.33* no   *4.41/3/49* unsure

26. If my friend had such wonderful news, I believe that s/he would probably contact me right away.

    81.94/89.53 yes   *5.73/3.49* no   *12.33/6.98* unsure

27. My best friend has seen me cry.

    95.15/78.82 yes   *4.85/21.18* no

28. I have seen my best friend cry.

    86.78/70.93 yes   *13.22/29.07* no

29. I can tell when my best friend is angry.

    95.59/96.51 yes   *.44/.00* no   *3.96/3.49* unsure

30. My best friend can tell when I'm angry.

    93.83/95.35 yes   *.88/.00* no   *5.29/4.65* unsure

31. I can tell when my friend is sad, upset, and/or distressed.

    98.65/95.29 yes   *.45/.00* no   *.90/4.71* unsure

32. My friend can tell when I'm sad, upset, and/or distressed.

    94.14/98.82 yes   *.90/.00* no   *4.95/1.18* unsure

33. When the relationship becomes demanding and confusing, I prefer to

    33.49/30.49 take some time away — alone

    12.26/6.10 spend time with others, but not my friend

    54.25/63.41 work it through with my friend

34. When the relationship becomes demanding and confusing, my friend prefers to

    32.54/23.75 take some time away — alone

    18.18/8.75 spend time with others, but not with me

    49.28/67.50 work it through with me

35. Imagine that you and your friend have just planned an event together, e.g., picnic, movie, tennis, dinner, etc., and you discover that your friend cannot keep the date. Your most typical response would be to (check only ONE)

    50.68/63.86 not go at all   *4.07/6.02* go alone

    45.25/30.12 call someone else

36. What do you suppose your friend would do if the tables were turned?
    44.55/54.22 not go at all   *6.82/8.43* go alone
    48.64/37.35 call someone else

37. I have told my best friend, "I love you."
    84.23/76.47 yes   *15.77/23.53* no

38. My best friend has said this to me.
    82.88/74.12 yes   *17.12/25.88* no

39. I am comfortable pursuing personal interests and hobbies apart from those I share with my best friend.
    99.10/100.00 yes   *.90/.00* no

40. My best friend becomes upset when I pursue personal interests and hobbies apart from what I share with her/him.
    5.41/.00 yes   *90.99/94.12* no   *3.60/5.88* unsure

41. My friend is comfortable pursuing personal interests and hobbies apart from those s/he shares with me.
    95.50/95.29 yes   *3.15/3.53* no   *1.35/1.18* unsure

42. I become upset when my friend pursues personal interests and hobbies apart from what s/he shares with me.
    1.36/.00 yes   *96.38/100.00* no   *2.26/.00* unsure

43. In my mind, the MOST intimate thing that my best friend and I do together is (check only ONE)
    8.11/12.20   have affectional/sexual contact
    .45/.00   give one another gifts
    1.35/2.44   travel together
    81.08/78.05   talk about what's important to us
    8.56/6.10   spend lots of time together
    .45/1.22   work together

44. If I discovered that my best friend and I were in a competitive situation for a job position, I probably would
    63.85/48.75 refuse to compete   *35.21/50.00* compete
    .94/1.25   ask my friend to withdraw

45. Based on my past experiences, if either I or my friend moved away, I suspect our relationship would
    72.57/61.18 remain as important to me years from now as it is now
    1.77/1.18   probably diminish over time and eventually terminate
    25.66/37.65 be important, but less so than now

46. When my best friend and I get together, we most frequently discuss (check ONE)

    3.62/13.10   our work

    17.65/16.67 things we're doing (events)

    78.73/70.24 our personal lives (feelings, values)

    .00/.00   events we shared in the past

47. When my friend and I argue, I find the one most likely to apologize first is

    26.61/22.22 me   *11.93/6.17* my friend

    61.47/71.60 we share this about equally

48. When my friend and I argue, I find that I

    24.89/22.62 withdraw   *.90/.00* stay with it until s/he wins

    73.76/77.38 stay with it until we reach a mutually satisfying conclusion

    .45/.00   stay with it until I win

49. In the above, my friend is most likely to

    15.91/9.64 withdraw   *.91/.00* stay with it until I win

    75.45/81.93 stay with it until we reach a mutually satisfying conclusion

    7.73/8.43   stay with it until s/he wins

50. In this relationship, I would say that (check only ONE)

    6.64/.00   we have several areas where we disagree, but just can't talk about them

    42.04/44.19 we have several areas in which we disagree, but we can talk about most of them

    50.88/55.81 we agree on just about everything, and we discuss those areas in which we disagree

    .44/.00   we always agree

51. When we get together to talk, the one most likely to introduce our topics of conversation is

    11.89/6.98 me   *15.42/17.44* my friend

    72.69/75.58 we share this about equally

52. When we get together, the one most likely to determine when we must "stop" (i.e., terminate) is

    16.30/18.60 me   *18.94/11.63* my friend

    64.76/69.77 we share this about equally

53. When my friend and I disagree on something, the one most likely to have the last word is

    14.16/4.76   me   *19.18/13.10*   my friend

    66.67/82.14   we share this about equally

54. My comfort level with "who gets the last word" is

    69.82/76.83   I'm okay

    18.92/18.29   I'm uncomfortable, and will probably bring it up for discussion

    11.26/4.88   I'm uncomfortable with it, but won't say anything

55. I feel that I truly respect and appreciate my best friend

    87.67/94.19   yes   *.88/.00*   no   *1.32/1.16*   unsure

    10.13/4.65   yes, but not as much as I'd like to

56. I feel that my best friend truly respects and appreciates me.

    91.59/96.51   yes   *1.33/.00*   no   *.44/1.16*   unsure

    6.64/2.33   yes, but not as much as I'd like

57. I feel that I really "listen" to my best friend when s/he talks.

    97.36/96.51   yes   *.44/.00*   no   *2.20/3.49*   unsure

58. I feel that my best friend really "listens" to me when I talk.

    92.07/94.19   yes   *.44/1.16*   no   *7.49/4.65*   unsure

59. My relational style is such that I (check only ONE)

    12.78/6.98   have one best friend at a time

    79.30/91.86 have a few (2–3) very close friends

    7.05/.00   have many acquaintances, none of whom are "best friends"

    .88/1.16   keep pretty much to myself

60. If I were asked to write my best friend's biography, I could probably do so.

    64.32/68.60   yes   *12.78/12.79*   no   *22.91/18.60*   unsure

61. If my best friend were asked to write my biography, s/he could probably do so.

    59.91/70.59   yes   *12.33/11.76*   no   *27.75/17.65*   unsure

62. The frequency of our talks at a "feeling" (gut-to-gut) level is (check ONE)

    73.13/77.91   about right for both of us

    14.10/5.81   enough for him/her, but not enough for me

    3.08/6.98   enough for me, but not enough for her/him

    9.69/9.30   inadequate for both of us

63. I know my best friend's financial situation.

    74.67/81.18 yes   *10.67/5.88* no   *14.67/12.94* unsure

64. My best friend knows my financial situation.

    78.22/78.82 yes   *9.33/7.06* no   *12.44/14.12* unsure

65. I believe that I know the most important events/concerns in my best friend's sexual history.

    48.67/65.48 yes   *27.88/21.43* no   *23.45/13.10* unsure

66. I believe that my best friend knows the most important events/concerns in my sexual history.

    49.78/63.53 yes   *36.56/27.06* no   *13.66/9.41* unsure

67. When my best friend and I discuss at a "feeling" level, the one who does the most self-disclosing is

    23.89/12.94 me   *12.83/10.59* my friend
    63.27/76.47 we share about equally

68. I estimate that I am fully self-disclosing (feelings, values) with my best friend about ____ percent of the time.

    3.96/2.35 less than 25   *12.33/10.59* about 25–50
    39.65/36.47 about 50–75   *44.05/50.59* more than 75

69. I estimate that my friend is fully self-disclosing with me about ____ percent of the time.

    6.61/3.53 less than 25   *13.66/16.47* about 25–50
    39.21/27.06 about 50–75   *40.53/52.94* more than 75

70. Overall, I would say that my relationship with this person is

    82.82/91.76 very satisfying and important to me
    14.54/8.24 somewhat satisfying and important to me
    2.64/.00 okay, but neither very satisfying nor important to me

71. I guess that my friend would say that our relationship is

    80.62/92.94 very satisfying and important to her/him
    18.50/7.06 somewhat satisfying and important to her/him
    .88/.00 okay, but neither very satisfying nor important to her/him

72. If it ever came to such a point, I think that I would die for my friend.

    47.35/56.47 yes   *3.98/4.71* no   *48.67/38.82* unsure

73. If it ever came to such a point, I think that my friend would die for me.

    44.25/56.47 yes   *4.87/5.88* no   *50.88/37.65* unsure

When you think about your current and past relationships, what do you find most important about them?

When you think about your current and past relationships, what do you find most difficult and/or bothersome about them?

Please feel free to use this space for any comments or elaborations about your friendships or your ideas about friendship.

Part II. Sexuality

This part of the study asks about your sexual involvements since entering religious life/diocesan clergy.

[It is not possible to provide percentages for all items because several respondents checked more than one item.]

1. I consider myself to be primarily
   87.01/72.16 heterosexual   *1.30/18.56* homosexual/lesbian
   11.69/9.28 ambisexual (bisexual)

2. Since making vows, I have engaged in behavior I would label "affectional."
   88.84/90.72 yes   *11.16/9.28* no

3. Since making vows, I have engaged in behavior I would label "sexual."
   48.93/61.86 yes   *51.07/38.14* no

(If NO, go to PART III)

4. Since making vows, I have been sexually involved with
   45.05/25.42 one person   *45.95/37.29* 2–3 people
   6.31/13.56 3–5 people   *2.70/23.73* more than 5 people

5. These partners have been
   38.74/31.67 exclusively male   *35.14/58.33* exclusively female
   7.21/6.67 mostly male   *5.41/3.33* mostly female
   13.51/.00 equally male and female

6. My partner(s) was (were) [check as many as apply]
   ____ married   ____ single   ____ divorced
   ____ vowed religious   ____ diocesan clergy

7. The approximate duration of my sexual involvement was
   ____ 1 or 2 episodes   ____ less than one year
   ____ 1–2 years   ____ 3–5 years   ____ more than five years

8. The impact of this behavior on my vowed life was (is)
   17.43/25.00 negligible
   47.71/41.67 to strengthen my commitment to my vocation
   6.42/15.00   to weaken my commitment to my vocation
   28.44/18.33 other

9. I became involved
   ____ by my own initiative
   ____ because of my partner's pressure
   ____ because both my partner and I agreed equally to it

10. For me, the most important aspect of the involvement was (check only ONE)
    95.45/76.67 the affectional experiences
    1.82/20.00   intercourse/orgasm/sexual arousal
    2.73/3.33   overall tension release

11. One or more of my partners was a close friend PRIOR to the physical involvement, but is no longer a close friend.
    ____ yes   ____ no

12. One or more of my partners has become a close friend SINCE the physical involvement.
    ____ yes   ____ no

13. One or more of these partners was a close friend prior to and has remained a close friend since the physical involvement.
    ____ yes   ____ no

14. One or more of these partners was not a good friend either before or after the physical involvement.
    ____ yes   ____ no

15. As far as I know, no one knows about these contacts unless I've told them.
    90.99/93.33 yes   *9.01/6.67* no

16. I have stopped such behavior in my life
    73.39/57.63 yes   *26.61/42.37* no

17. I stopped such behavior primarily because (check only ONE)
    42.00/43.64 I chose to; I was uncomfortable with it
    2.00/.00   my partner chose to; s/he was uncomfortable with it
    34.00/16.36 we decided together to stop
    1.00/1.82   we didn't want to stop but had to because of actual or threatened censure
    21.00/38.18 I haven't stopped being sexually active

18. My overall feeling about my experience is (check only ONE)
    6.48/5.00   I feel guilty and wish I hadn't gotten involved
    45.37/33.33 I feel guilty but am grateful for what I learned
    33.33/31.67 I feel no guilt but choose not to repeat the behavior
    14.81/30.00 I feel no guilt and will probably opt for the behavior again

19. The majority of my sexual contacts were initiated by
    4.67/20.34   me   *36.45/11.86* my partner
    58.88/67.80 both of us about equally.

Please use this space to add any comments about your own sexual involvements or your attitudes about them.

Part III. Celibacy

This part of the study asks about your opinions and attitudes about celibacy.

1. Which of the following best reflects your understanding of the reason for celibacy (check only ONE)
    29.46/13.04 spouse of Christ
    7.59/28.26   requirement of my ministry
    45.98/36.96 availability for ministry
    16.96/21.74 countercultural statements

2. Which of the following best reflects your belief about celibate living.
    .00/.00   avoid people as much as possible to avoid temptation
    2.59/3.13   mix with people, but keep it professional and distant
    7.76/12.50   pursue friendships, but avoid any affection or touch
    86.21/73.96 pursue friendships and be appropriately affectionate, even if it might lead to physical involvement — it's worth the risk — but make every effort to be celibate
    3.45/8.33   it's okay to be sexually active while committed to celibacy as long as the relationship is sincere/intimate AND neither ministry nor community suffer
    .00/2.08   it's okay to be sexually active with anyone I choose provided I don't give scandal and don't neglect my ministerial/community responsibilities

3. I believe that celibacy for diocesan clergy should be optional.
    89.61/89.58 yes   *10.39/10.42* no

4. If I knew a vowed celibate friend of mine was sexually active, I would probably say something to her/him.

   26.50/40.00 yes   *26.92/24.21* no   *46.58/35.79* unsure

5. I believe that diocesan priests and men and women religious who are sexually active should be reported to authorities/superiors.

   9.55/21.11 yes   *90.45/78.89* no

6. In my opinion, celibacy is more often a goal than a reality for the majority of vowed celibates.

   25.11/43.48 yes   *74.89/56.52* no

7. In my opinion, celibates are faithful to their vow as long as they do not engage in heterosexual intercourse.

   13.54/15.79 I agree   *86.46/84.21* I disagree

8. I believe that it is possible for some people to be sexually active and committed celibates at the same time.

   30.49/34.04 yes   *69.51/65.96* no

9. My training in sexuality and celibacy PRIOR to vowing celibacy was
   54.15/51.55 pretty negligible
   23.58/13.40 basic biology; not much else
   12.23/12.37 lots of biology, but little values exploration
   10.04/22.68 both strong biology and extensive values exploration

10. My training in sexuality and celibacy SINCE vowing celibacy has been
    23.48/21.65 pretty negligible
    4.35/4.12 basic biology; not much else
    8.26/6.19 lots of biology but little values exploration
    63.91/68.04 both strong biology and extensive values exploration

11. The majority of my information in sexuality and celibacy came from
    ____ classroom presentations   ____ personal reading
    ____ workshops   ____ discussion

Please use this space to write in any additional comments or observations about celibacy.

May I quote you on your "write in" comments (anonymously, of course)?
     ____ yes   ____ no

NOTES

Introduction

1. See Donald J. Goergen, *The Power of Love* (Chicago: Thomas More Press, 1979), for a discussion of the five loves of self-esteem, friendship, community, ministry, and prayer.

2. See Rollo May, *Power and Innocence* (New York: W. W. Norton and Co., 1972).

3. See Donald J. Goergen, "Self-Love, Self-Knowledge, and True Humility," *Spirituality Today* 34 (1982): 155–65.

4. See Donald J. Goergen, "Presence to God, Presence to the World: Spirituality," *The Praxis of Christian Experience: An Introduction to the Theology of Edward Schillebeeckx*, ed. Robert Schreiter and Mary Catherine Hilkert (San Francisco: Harper & Row, 1989), 86–100.

5. See Donald J. Goergen, *The Power of Love*, 192–266.

6. See, e.g., Donald J. Goergen, ibid.; Wilkie Au, *By Way of the Heart: Toward a Holistic Christian Spirituality* (New York: Paulist Press, 1989).

Chapter 1: The Story

1. Sheila Murphy, *Midlife Wanderer: The Woman Religious in Midlife Transition* (Mystic, Conn.: Twenty-third Publications, 1983).

2. An exhaustive listing of all these sources is beyond the scope of this discussion. However, some of the references that will be cited in subsequent chapters include (in alphabetical order): Janet Hyde, *Half the Human Experience*, 3d ed. (Lexington, Mass.: Heath, 1985); Linda Lindsey, *Gender Roles* (Englewood Cliffs, N.J.: Prentice Hall, 1990); Michael McGill, *The McGill Report: On Male Intimacy* (New York: Harper & Row, 1986); Stuart Miller, *Men and Friendship* (Boston: Houghton Mifflin, 1983); Janice Raymond, *A Passion for Friends: Toward A Philosophy of Female Affection* (Boston: Beacon Press, 1987); Lillian Rubin, *Intimate Strangers* (New York: Harper & Row, 1984); and *Just Friends* (New York: Harper & Row, 1986); Anne Schaef, *Women's Reality* (Minneapolis: Winston Press, 1981).

3. The most commonly cited source is Daniel Levinson, *The Seasons of a Man's Life* (New York: Ballantine Books, 1978). The same finding was popularized by Gail Sheehy in her *Passages* (New York: E. P. Dutton, 1974).

4. Women's intimacy patterns are well presented by Janice Raymond, *A Passion for Friends*. Women's connectedness in the moral realm is discussed by Carol Gilligan in her *In a Different Voice* (Cambridge, Mass.: Harvard University Press, 1982).

5. Janet Hyde, *Understanding Human Sexuality*, 4th ed. (New York: McGraw-Hill, 1990).

6. This broader definition was originally articulated by Donald Goergen in *The Sexual Celibate* (New York: Image Books, 1979).

7. Sandra Bem, *Bem Sex Role Inventory* (Palo Alto, Calif.: Consulting Psychologists Press, Inc., 1981).

8. For a summary of these, see Hyde, *Half the Human Experience*.

9. Jean Alvarez, "Psychological Androgyny among Catholic Sisters," doctoral dissertation, University of Northern Colorado, 1978.

10. For those interested in the technical side of the story, I used a Digital Rainbow 100 computer and Microstat software (1983, 1984) by Ecosoft, Inc., of Indianapolis, Ind.

11. This age difference is statistically significant. A further breakdown of the final sample for women is 25 percent between ages 35 and 45 (n = 58), 44 percent between ages 45 and 55 (n = 104), and 31 percent between ages 55 and 65 (n = 74). Details of the men's group came to 41 percent between ages 35 and 45 (n = 40), 39 percent between ages 45 and 55 (n = 38), and 20 percent between ages 55 and 65 (n = 19).

Chapter 2: Intriguing Intimacy

1. Michael McGill, *The McGill Report: On Male Intimacy* (New York: Harper & Row, 1986); Lillian Rubin, *Intimate Strangers* (New York: Harper & Row, 1984).

2. Anne Schaef, *Women's Reality* (Minneapolis: Winston Press, 1981), and Janice Raymond, *A Passion for Friends: Toward A Philosophy of Female Affection* (Boston: Beacon Press, 1987). Raymond specifically cites women's religious communities as environments where true intimacy could flourish. Another researcher who sees intimacy as vulnerability is Gilligan, *In a Different Voice* (Cambridge, Mass.: Harvard University Press, 1982).

3. Betty Berzon, *Permanent Partners* (New York: E. P. Dutton, 1988), 93.

4. Daniel Levinson, *The Seasons of a Man's Life* (New York: Ballantine Books, 1978).

5. The differences were statistically significant at $p = .05$ or less using Chi-square analysis both with and without correction factor.

6. Schaef, *Women's Reality*; McGill, *The McGill Report*.

7. Stuart Miller, *Men and Friendship* (Boston: Houghton Mifflin, 1983), 191–92. Following his divorce, Stuart Miller was lonely and disorganized. He realized he did not have any close male friends and undertook a personal study to discover why he, and so many other men, lacked strong male relationships. He interviewed almost 1,000 people in the U.S. and six European countries and found that men were, simply, afraid of friendship. He suggests that men engage so little with other men because they fear both the commitment and the vulnerability; calling another male to help with housepainting or moving projects proves too much to many men. He laments that men often hide behind the smoke screen of work responsibilities and family demands when the risk of true male friendship threatens their independence. He concedes that men have much to learn about intimacy from women, and urges them to break down the walls that isolate them from one another:

> The relationship is its own context. Friendship may arise from another relationship — work, for example — but it is not dependent upon it. Male friendship is just one man and another. Yet so many friendships break up or attenuate into nothing when commonplace interest or work are no longer shared. It means that men have not had the essential friendship.... A man's high voltage engagement with another man, each of whom has a daily place in the other's inner being — from such inwardness all necessary, dignified, and pleasant actions can grow.

Chapter 3: Sexual, Celibate, or Sexual Celibate?

1. Numerous sources discuss this in much greater detail. For a general history of Western religious attitudes, see Janet Hyde, *Understanding Human Sexuality*, 4th ed. (New York: McGraw-Hill, 1990), esp. chap. 22. An excellent historical sketch of attitudes in general regarding sexuality is presented in chapter 1 of *Human Sexuality*, 3d ed. by William Masters, Virginia Johnson, and Robert Kolodny (Boston: Scott, Foresman, and Company, 1988). A very fine analysis of Christian thought from both Scripture and tradition is presented by Donald Goergen, *The Sexual Celibate* (New York: Image Books, 1979), esp. chap. 1.

2. Joan Timmerman, *The Mardi Gras Syndrome* (New York: Crossroad, 1984).

3. An excellent explication and critique of this is presented by Rosemary Ruether in her chapter "Homophobia, Heterosexism, and Pastoral

Practice," in *Homosexuality in the Priesthood and Religious Life*, ed. Jeannine Gramick (New York: Crossroad, 1989).

4. Alfred Kinsey, W. B. Pomeroy, and C. E. Martin, *Sexual Behavior in the Human Male* (Philadelphia: Saunders, 1948); Alfred Kinsey, W. B. Pomeroy, C. E. Martin, and P. H. Gebhard, *Sexual Behavior in the Human Female* (Philadelphia: Saunders, 1948).

5. Hyde, *Understanding Human Sexuality*, esp. chap. 15.

6. James Wolf, ed., *Gay Priests* (New York: Harper & Row, 1989).

7. A. W. Richard Sipe, *A Secret World: Sexuality and the Search for Celibacy* (New York: Brunner/Mazel, 1990).

8. Hyde, *Understanding Human Sexuality*, esp. chap. 16.

9. Gramick, *Homosexuality in the Priesthood and Religious Life*.

10. This point is stressed by Ruether in "Homophobia, Heterosexism, and Pastoral Practice."

11. Sandra Schneiders, *New Wineskins* (New York: Paulist, 1986), 103–4.

12. Ibid., 105.

13. Pamela Bjorklund, Ph.D., personal communication, May 27, 1991.

Chapter 4: Personality Types and the Road to Relationships

1. Jean Alvarez, "Psychological Androgyny among Catholic Sisters," doctoral dissertation, University of Northern Colorado, 1978.

2. Lillian Rubin's most recent book, *Erotic Wars* (New York: Farrar, Straus, and Giroux, 1990), is an excellent analysis, complete with her own empirical research, of the sexual and gender revolutions and the impact of both on women and men today. A 1991 paperback edition of the book is available (Torch Books, New York).

3. Inge Broverman, D. C. Broverman, F. E. Clarkson, P. S. Rosenkrantz, and S. R. Vogel, "Sex Role Stereotypes and Clinical Judgments of Mental Health," *Journal of Consulting and Clinical Psychology* 34:1–7.

4. A brief review of various research findings is reported in Janet Hyde, *Half the Human Experience*, 3d ed. (Lexington, Mass.: Heath, 1985), chap. 14. An excellent and very readable book addressing women's concerns and their treatment by various professionals is Karen Johnson and Tom Ferguson, *Trusting Ourselves: The Sourcebook on Psychology for Women* (New York: Atlantic Monthly Press, 1990). The notes at the end of each chapter are packed with references to the most recent research. Finally, that attitudes among mental health providers toward women had not changed over the years was reported by T. L. Ruble in a 1983 article, "Issues of Change in the 1970s," *Sex Roles* 9 (1983): 397–401.

5. James Doyle, *The Male Experience*, 2d ed. (Dubuque, Ia.: Wm. C. Brown Publishers, 1989).

6. Carol Gilligan in her *In a Different Voice* (Cambridge, Mass.: Harvard University Press, 1982); Anne Schaef, *Women's Reality* (Minneapolis: Winston Press, 1981). Also, Nancy Chodorow, *The Reproduction of Mothering* (Berkeley: University of California Press, 1978). Additional summaries can be found in Hyde, *Half the Human Experience*.

7. Sandra Schneiders, *Beyond Patching: Faith and Feminism in the Catholic Church* (New York: Paulist, 1991), 79–80, explains:

> The dichotomous dualism between male divine creator and female natural creation within which the male human is assimilated to the divine sphere and the female human to the natural sphere is the paradigm for the endless series of superior/inferior dichotomies that is characterized by masculine/feminine. Thus, at the male pole are divine creativity, power, intelligence, initiative, activity, goodness, independence, and at the female pole are natural passivity, weakness, instinct and emotionality, receptivity, evil, dependence. The shorthand cipher for this pervasive dualism is the spirit/body dichotomy, spirit representing everything divine and body representing everything natural. The spirit is male; the body is female. Culture is the triumph of male spirit over female nature.

8. Some examples of instruments with traditionally based M-F scales are the Minnesota Multiphasic Personality Inventory, the California Psychological Inventory, and the Guilford-Zimmerman Temperament Survey.

9. Any general textbook on psychological testing published within the past ten years should provide an overview of research data on M-F scales and their correlations to career interests and emotional health and adjustment.

10. Margaret Mead, *Sex and Temperament in Three Primitive Societies* (New York: William Morrow, 1935).

11. Sandra Bem, *Bem Sex Role Inventory* (Palo Alto, Calif.: Consulting Psychologists Press, Inc., 1981).

12. Other scoring systems have been developed by J. T. Spence, R. Helmreich, and J. Stapp, "Ratings of Self and Peers on Sex-Role Attributes and Their Relation to Self-Esteem and Conceptions of Masculinity and Femininity," *Journal of Personality and Social Psychology* 32 (1975): 29–39. See also F. Strahan, "Remarks on Bem's Measurement of Psychological Androgyny: Alternatives, Methods and a Supplementary Analysis," *Journal of Consulting and Clinical Psychology* 43 (1975): 568–71. See the *Manual* of the *Bem* for a more complete explanation.

13. Sandra Bem herself, despite her years' investment developing and pursuing androgyny studies, now questions the efficacy of her own earlier

work. See her article, "Gender Schema Theory and Its Implications for Child Development: Raising Gender-Aschematic Children in a Gender-Schematic Society," *Signs* 8 (1983): 598–616. It is important to note that Bem's earlier findings, in and of themselves, are not invalidated by her later thinking on the topic.

14. Sandra Bem, "Probing the Promise of Androgyny," *The Psychology of Women: Ongoing Debates*, ed. Mary Roth Walsh (New Haven: Yale University Press, 1987), 206–25.

15. "What this pattern suggests to me is that the major effect of femininity in women — untempered by a sufficient level of masculinity — may not be to inhibit instrumental or masculine behaviors, per se, but to inhibit any behavior at all in a situation where the 'appropriate' behavior is left ambiguous or unspecified" (ibid., 221).

16. I distributed the short form hand-scored edition of the *Bem* and used the split-median method of scoring. See the *Manual* for a more detailed explanation.

17. Scoring criteria for assigning psychological type on the *Bem:*

Androgynous:	both scores at or above cut-off
Feminine:	only femininity score at or above cut-off
Masculine:	only masculinity score at or above cut-off
Undifferentiated:	both scores below cut-off

18. Significant at the $p < .05$ level.

19. Another way of presenting the data is to report the percentages of men and women who came out androgynous, feminine, masculine, and undifferentiated in a frequency distribution. I spoke with Jeannine Gramick, SSND, who is, in addition to many other professional identities, a professional mathematician. She advised me to work with group means rather than with frequency distributions because they are statistically stronger and clearer (Personal communication, June 30, 1991).

Chapter 5: Predictability within the Chaos

1. This is not to suggest that women and men in general are not equally concerned. In fact, having discussed these findings with lay women and men, I've learned that many of the results can be applied to the general population.

2. Any general textbook of developmental psychology covers this material.

3. General social psychology texts routinely publish chapters on interpersonal attraction.

4. Mark Knapp, *Social Intercourse: From Greeting to Good-bye* (Boston: Allyn and Bacon, Inc., 1978).

5. Patrick Malone, and Thomas Malone, *The Art of Intimacy* (Englewood Cliffs, N.J.: Prentice-Hall, 1987).

6. Both of Harriet Lerner's books describe relational dysfunction and offer suggestions for change. See *The Dance of Anger* (New York: Harper & Row, 1985), and *The Dance of Intimacy* (New York: Harper & Row, 1989).

7. Daniel Levinson, *The Seasons of a Man's Life* (New York: Ballantine Books, 1978); Sheila Murphy, *Midlife Wanderer: The Woman Religious in Midlife Transition* (Mystic, Conn.: Twenty-third Publications, 1983).

8. See Levinson, *The Seasons of a Man's Life,* and Murphy, *Midlife Wanderer.*

9. Time estimates vary, but Levinson's generalized framework of four years is accepted by many as a workable "guesstimate" of the process.

10. Jeannine Gramick, "Lesbian Nuns in Midlife Transition," *CMI Journal* (1990): 32.

Chapter 6: Relational Emergence over Time

1. Sean Sammon, *Alcoholism's Children: ACoAs in Priesthood and Religious Life* (New York: Alba House, 1989). The classic in this field is Janet Woititz, *Adult Children of Alcoholics* (Pompano Beach, Fla.: Health Communications, 1983).

2. Ellen Bass and Laura Davis, *The Courage to Heal: A Guide for Women Survivors of Child Sexual Abuse* (New York: Harper & Row, 1988). A similar book written for male adult survivors is Mike Lew, *Victims No Longer: Men Recovering from Incest and Other Sexual Child Abuse* (New York: Harper & Row, 1988).

3. Sheila Murphy and Mary Jakubiak, "Incest Survivors in Women's Religious Communities," *Human Development* 8, no. 2 (1987): 19–25.

4. This insight comes from Barbara Hammrel, OP, a pastoral counselor who works with adult survivors.

5. Joan Ohanneson, *Woman Survivor in the Church* (Minneapolis: Winston Press, 1980); see 159–62 for the complete prayer.